5AM

Wake UP! Shake it OFF! Get UP! Show UP! Level UP! Wrap it UP!

SAMSON YUNG-ABU

Copyright © 2023 Samson Yung-Abu

All rights reserved, including the right to reproduce this book, or portions thereof in any form. No part of this text may be reproduced, transmitted, downloaded, decompiled, reverse engineered, or stored, in any form or introduced into any information storage and retrieval system, in any form or by any means, whether electronic or mechanical without the express written permission of the author.

The views expressed in this work are solely those of the author and do not necessarily reflect the views of the publisher, and the publisher hereby disclaims any responsibility for them.

ISBN: 978-1-916696-18-1

PublishNation
www.publishnation.co.uk

The author has an undergraduate degree in law & criminology, a postgraduate degree in general law, a law school in Berlin certificate, and a MSc degree in psychology. The author is a life-long creator turned tutor who enjoys motivating people across the world, teaching and inspiring others about the joys of life and education.

Why?

To change your reality, you must change your mentality. To do so, we start with the word why.

I believe that there is a mental pandemic that is going around at the moment. One that has been around for a while but now seems beyond our control. This mental pandemic is called **The unconscious rushing-around mentality**. The unconscious rushing-around mentality expresses the belief that we have become mindless people in life rushing around to do too much with a body, mind, and soul that isn't designed to just DO. We wake up each day with the mindset that we must get there, we must do this or we must respond to that. We barely stop anymore to experience any conscious thinking, feel anything pleasant or be at peace. But, what happens when we rush? We crash. We burn out. We stress out. We become overwhelmed and feel unappreciated. We become deprived of a quality healthy lifestyle because things are done without heart, without thinking, and at the very least, things are often left unfinished. But, there is a cure, and it is called 5 AM.

One day, during my mentoring sessions, I asked a group of students, who in the room wanted to be successful. They all raised their hands. Good. You are in the right room, I thought.

"Who in this room gets up at 5am?" Heads went down, and no hands were raised. "Why, does none of you get up at 5am?"

"Because it is difficult," one said swiftly.

"Because I hate it," said another.

"Because it is insane," someone at the back uttered.

"Because it is an inconvenient time and I am not a morning person," one said, and a few agreed more and nodded in agreement.

"I need my sleep. I won't be able to get through the day waking up at that early!" one exclaimed.

"Those are fair and sincere justifications, I can also relate. I mean, I used to buy into this logic some years back," I added. "But here is the thing, none of you said it was impossible to wake up at 5am. And rightfully so."

Previously at the crack of dawn, my body often felt like a diamond, too heavy to move in my bed. My arms usually look at their longest, so no matter how further from my bed I kept my alarm clock, my hand found the snooze button. My cheap and thin mattress felt like soapstone, and my warm blanket felt like the soft hands of a masseur. Physically, mentally and emotionally, it felt almost impossible to get out of bed! But, there is no such thing as impossible when it comes to getting up at 5am to positively change a life that isn't working. We are capable of waking up and getting up before 5am if we want to. So it is possible. And what's possible is always doable, even if it is an inconvenience or deeply not preferable.

We must be aware that our justifications against doing what's possible are a dangerous way to self-sabotage our chances of living our best life. Easy never changes misery. Change does not come easy, otherwise, no one who has achieved greatness would be proud of themselves for achieving it. Easy is doing the mundane: brushing your teeth. Taking a shower. Washing the pots. There is no excellence through easy. Easy don't bring reward, neither does complaining, blaming, escaping or ignoring. At most easy gives us relief. But a temporal one, till we have to repeat the same thing again and again. Easy is the art of operating at a mediocre level. And once we get into the habit of operating at a mediocre level, we can only achieve what is below our means and power.

My personal excuses for not wanting to wake up early before I started doing so were as follows: I will wake up late because I have the rest of the day to be awake. I will sleep longer because I function better when I have had enough. I can't wake up as early as 5am because I get so moody throughout the day, and I get so tired that I don't want to do anything, and everything just stresses me out.

But the reality of the matter was that I just wanted to ensure that I had as much sleep as possible before I had to go to work. I woke up for work, not for my life. And I had less to show for being a workaholic in my life. In retrospect, I realised that my lack of more hours to sleep wasn't making me moody, but my lack in life was what was making me moody, sad and frustrated.

Once I decided that waking up at 5am had great benefits, I quickly realised that each day is not just for us to be awake. It is for us to be alive. What's the difference between being awake and alive? You might ask. Being awake is opening your eyes. Being alive is being able to do everything else the dead can't do while being awake.

What changed for me before anything changed was understanding why getting up earlier than ever before mattered. So, it began with a why.

"Why do I have to get up at this ungodly hour?" I asked myself one day.

"Well, I am sick of the life I am in. I know I can do better. I know I can have better. I know I can feel happier, calmer, and healthier. I want to improve and grow. And, me having enough sleep to function isn't really doing it, is it?" I said to myself against the mirror. "I mean, my days are still fruitless despite having enough sleep, at times an extra few hours in bed. When I am awake, I am still tired anyways. Still moody, sad, and distracted."

All I ever achieved was that I functioned better at failing over and over again. And yes, sleeping longer felt nice. But my reality was a complete mass of mess. That had to change, and it started with changing my mentality.

What time we choose to wake up is a matter of preference, and therefore a matter of mindset. And the simple, harsh truth is this; we are not night owls or morning people. Our life choices determine when we are more productive and less effective. When we were young kids, for example, our parents made us go to bed at night time and we woke up in the morning just fine for school. On holidays, we woke up before everyone else. Excited, and expectant. Eager and energised. Then, we weren't night owls. We were just people with fewer economic and social burdens. So, truth be told, we are not born night owls. We just live in a corporate world that decides our waking and sleeping pattern. The ability to evolve our minds is in our DNA. The ability to modify our body is in our DNA. The ability to adapt to our surroundings is in our DNA. We have all we need for any lifestyle change. We just have to want to change. In other words, as humans, the ability to change is our superpower.

Before I became a writer before I became a CEO. I worked evenings and overnight shifts for many years. I don't anymore. Now, I mainly work during the day. And I find myself at my happiest, and healthiest. And I never failed to get up at 5 am daily. So, on this note, *we are not who we think we are only when the time finally becomes convenient. We are not who we think we are only when our job closes for the day. We are not free when we are allowed out. We are free when we allow ourselves out. We are not free when we are told when to be free. We are free when the time we are set free to live our life is of our choice.*

So, whoever has the power to choose has the power of freedom. 5am is definitely for those who have the power to choose to wake up before the time the corporate world wants them to do so. If you haven't been happy lately. If you have been under so much pressure lately. If you've felt stuck and held back lately. If your mind is in a mess lately, this tells me that you feel out of control of the world around you. Try waking up at 5 am. Make your progress more personal.

For me, waking up at 5 am is a personal affair for anyone out there who wishes to reclaim their life, and take it to the next level. Waking up at 5 am might not be for everyone, but it is for anyone who is fed up with how they feel and how they live their life currently. 5am is not about being praised by society. It is about you being proud of yourself for being different and disciplined. It is not about being more productive than anyone. It is about being at peace with you. It is about finding sustainable focus, and clarity. It is about strengthening your self-control, self-restraint, self-resilience, and self-reliance. For me, 5 am has been a great tool that has aided me in reevaluating my schedule, reconstructing my daily to-do list, and reorganising my social calendar in a way that impacts my lifestyle positively.

So, for me, getting up at 5am has been a life-changing, long-term habit. It has been one of the greatest ways to prove to myself that I am serious about changing my life for the better. You see, when you want more for your life, when you genuinely say, *I am done with my old self and my old life, and this is the life that I want now*, you wake up differently. You wake up before anyone you know. You wake up energised and excited. You don't just wake up whenever you do; you wake up with an alarm clock, with intent, ready to give yourself the best life you can have. And when your alarm clock goes off, you don't grunt, you don't complain, you don't hesitate, you don't resist, but instead, you insist on getting up before you can even think about pressing that snooze button.

I never miss setting my alarm clock and waking up early. I never miss a sunrise. I never miss a sunset. Therefore, I never miss the full power and potential of each day. When the day brightens, I am up. When the day fades into darkness, I am still there. I stay present, and I never miss the day's worth. That's why I get more out of the day. That is how you can start using the day to your advantage.

But here is the most important thing about waking up each day: *it's one thing to wake up, and it is another thing to show up fired up, ready to get to work and make the day count positively.* How do we achieve that? I asked myself one day, fed up and ready to give up on my goals. The answer is this: *We wake up and start the day by thinking positively about ourselves and about how we want the day to start and finish.*

As expressed above, for many people, waking up early is hard. Waking up early is impossible. Waking up early is not their thing. However, this is not because they don't have the ability to wake up early. It is because they don't have the drive to get up when they do wake up early. But to those who want more out of life, to those whose lives need a positive makeover, waking up isn't what they must fix. THAT IS THE EASY PART. The challenging part is this: it is not just about waking up motivated or waking up excited, but it is about shaking off that sense of tiredness. It is about getting up, fired up, showing up fearlessly and in a state of wellness and then wrapping the day up purposely, positively, and productively by all means necessary. It is not opening your eyes that counts the most, but opening your mind to the possibility of your success happening when you get up and work hard.

The rich don't have a watch with more than 12 numbers on it. And neither do the poor, the unhealthy, nor the unintelligent. When it comes to time, we are dealt with equal cards. It is how we prioritise and play our cards that matter. It is how we use our card that makes the difference, that differentiates the few who consider themselves winners from those who find themselves far from winning in life. Creating time for ourselves is so paramount. Time is one of the most important nutrients for growth and happiness. Without the involvement of time, transformation cannot exist. The same goes for every area of our life. Where we invest time, there we harvest. Everything else dies through neglect.

Why Does It Have to Be Five in the Morning? Can't It Be Late at Night?

To get the freshest fruits, to take home the sweetest and ripest fruits, you must be at the marketplace before the crowd awakens.

Well, sometimes, I call 5am the ripe hour: It is the hour that you can enjoy your time fully undisturbed. A time when the human worms of life haven't started crawling out of their shelter to fest on you with their needs, wants, expectations, and desires. It is the hour that your peace taste the most satisfactory. A time, your dreams taste the sweetest just thinking about them. A time that your mind feels supercharged, spacious, and special. A time when your heart beats without worry or hurry. To me, 5am, like a ripe fruit, is the sweetest hour of the day.

"*But waking up at 5am might deprive me of my sleep?*" We might argue. But, as you read on, it will make sense as to why sleeping for too long is overrated and why there are other more deadly things to conquer than a lack of a few more hours of sleep. Besides, you can sleep all you want, but when you wake up, your problems will be right where you left them. Your life will be just as sad as it was before you slept. You see, the deepest or longest sleep time can't cure the darkest point in your life. You can't sleep your pain away. You can't sleep your health conditions away. You can't sleep the minus in your bank account away. You can't sleep a broken relationship away. You can't sleep being jobless away. In fact, unlike a lack of 7/8 hours of sleep, research has been able to link a deep level of sadness to suicide. Sadness kills people. Sadness leads to suicide. Sleep doesn't cure sadness. Sleep doesn't diminish sadness. Early rise on the other hand has a greater potential to resolve our problems.

If we cared to think about it, it isn't hard to figure out a few other reasons as to why waking up as early as 5am might benefit our entire life. There are articles all over the internet to provide us with answers as to why.

The most obvious reasons anyone would want to get up early are perhaps for medical emergencies. Perhaps because no other alternative means of transportation other than a lift is available. Maybe to beat the rush of traffic, for deadlines that need to be met within a very short period of time, or simply just to get more personal chores done because one is going on a vacation.

They say successful people wake up early, often at 5AM and no later than 6am. But the benefits of waking up at 5am are not just for entrepreneurs or CEOs, but also for people who wish to be happy, calm, relaxed, well rested, and at peace within themselves.

Personally, apart from the economic gain and being able to get more done, waking up earlier than usual has helped me create a healthier habit. When it comes to my health and physical fitness I usually call 5am the **Sniper's Hour** to kill it: To pull the trigger on some silent but effective exercise. This is simply because in our modern lifestyle when it comes to personal growth, 5am provides a distinct window of opportunity like no other time of the day. At 5am, it is just you and your target: YOU. There is no human interruption or distractions in my proximity, neither is anyone else aware of my presence during such a silent period. The space is all mine, and the silence is my ally. My primary job is to focus and hit the target: growth.

It should follow that waking up as early as 5am, while it includes economical/financial benefits; it is also beneficial to personal wellness, specifically to emotional, mental and physical growth. 5am is a major keystone habit as to why world-class people are world-class people in their respective fields of choice. They are the only groups of people that wake up consistently and purposely before daybreak, and before every average person does. They tend to have a full experience of each day. They tend to capture the beauty of each day like no other.

However, the same cannot be said about the average person. Most average people stay average because they put themselves last each day. This is why they tend to believe that they are most productive at night time. During the day, they have no time, nor the energy for self-improvement, and self-discovery. Surprisingly, the average person tends to be able to summon the time, and energy to watch the news, for online platforms, digital distractions, family, boss, socialising, and so on. In other words, once they've met those daily self-imposed obligations, later on as the day fades into finality, they now have time to stay focused: they suddenly become a productive person. *"I am a night person,"* they tend to say. This is the average person's language that translates to this: *I have nothing else to do now. I am now free.*

However, the average person does not ascent to greatness by being a night person. It is not when we have nothing else to do that we must feel capable or ready to act on making positive changes in our life. It is when we have much to do, but decide that we come first before anything else gets done, that is when self-development begins to flourish at a rate that goes beyond the average person's reach.

Unlike world-class individuals, the average person tends to have a poor experience of each day and often tends to capture the crumbs and grunts of the day. The average person does not wake up and feel the sunlight, take a calm breath, and expect a smooth and joyful experience of the day. The average person wakes up and feels stressed about life and takes deep worrying breaths, wondering what might possibly go wrong today.

So, if you want to be happy, calm, at peace, and never in a rush, then wake up early, not late. Below are my logical reasons as to why you getting up as early as 5am will transform you and your life for the better as it did mine.

At 5am You Get You First before Everyone Else Takes from You

Getting up before everyone means one very important thing: ***First present, receives first***. In other words, you are the first to get from you. Unlike at night time, once everyone is done needing you, using you, abusing you, bleeding you, and overworking you, at 5am, you are not giving yourself what's left of you: ***the broken you, the drained you, the tired you, the stressed out you, or the fed up you.*** You are not giving yourself the least of you. You are giving yourself the first of you. The best of you. The untainted you. The peaceful you. You are giving yourself the first of your thought. The first of your grace. The first of your heartbeat. You really can't have the best in life or be the first at anything if all you are willing to give yourself is what's left of you by the end of the day.

5am Provides the Certainty of Peace and Quietness

5am is my out-of-life hour, similar to the out-of-office hour. It is a time where no emergency is an emergency except the one I create for myself. It is a time I am most certain that nobody can reach me but me. It is a time when I am certain my neighbour who enjoys watching TV at a loud volume is sleeping, and a time when my other neighbours aren't up for anything. It is a time any of my family members aren't tip-toeing to get a late-night or early-morning snack. Knowing that there is a time no one would jump out of bed unless the building is burning is a great awareness tool to create a sustainable growth routine. This logical awareness helped me maintain a guaranteed routine that I never needed to adjust to accommodate anyone at any time.

5am Provides You with a Sense of Delight

Previously when I woke up, I already felt down and miserable because I was getting up to get ready for work straight away. My emotion was already negative because I was about to go to a place where I rather not be. Not because it was a bad place or an unbearable place to be, but because I was still physically drained, mentally overwhelmed, generally stressed out, worried about my personal life, feeling hopeless and everything negative added to it. I am sure most of us feel that way right now. We feel like we can't even catch a breath. One minute we were at work, and now it feels like we are heading back there without any break or breaths taken in between.

When was the last time you felt delighted just after you got up? For me, it is now every day. The awareness that I am doing what my old self wouldn't dare do before makes me delighted and proud.

It is one thing to be proud of what you've achieved or are working towards, and it is another thing to be delighted with what you are currently doing differently to get it. There is something to be delighted about when waking up at a time you never thought you would ever agree to. That in itself makes you alive and joyful. Often we assume that we are incapable of getting up early even if we know the benefits. When you are genuinely serious enough about changing your life for the better, y**our** *no way I am waking up this early* becomes **your** *nothing will get in my way of getting up this morning.*

So, once we do start getting up at 5am, we begin to experience the discovery of a deep sense of self-capability and commitment. This is why the sight of yourself doing what you thought you couldn't do brings a kind of joy that makes you say, *Wow, it is 5am! And I am up! Is this really me, up at this early hour of the day! It really is! I am delighted.*

You Are at Your Best at 5am

Whether you like it or not, your best chance at working on all cylinders is at 5am. At night time, mentally, emotionally or physically, you are already in a disinterested and disengaging state of mind. At night time, you are already worn out by other day's activities and events, be it virtually or in the real world. You might not notice it, but the day does take a toll on us at night time. The constant screen time, the constant family time, the constant worrying time, they all add up. *But I am a night owl, and everyone usually goes to bed at night time, so I am free to work then*, some might argue. Yes, but your social media is awake and alive because there are people around the world posting at that time, and you can't stay off it. *But, I work best at night*, some might also say. That's to say, *I get more jobs done at that time*. But, it is not about what time you work best, but about what time is the best time to start achieving more in your life. We can't change others. We can't make others lock themselves in their room so we can work in a peaceful non-distractive environment. But who gets up early other than those who wish to achieve more in life? Not those who have no purpose. But you do! So, 5am is for you. Our body clock can be adjusted to accommodate our new early waking habit. We just have to believe in it and buy into it.

You Are Most Attentive and Productive at 5am

Take note: ***The best time to catch prey is when it is not being chased by other hunters.*** There is a moment during your day when everyone starts wanting you: your time, your skillset, your affection, your care, your brain, your advice. All of which require you to give your attention and usefulness. All of which you need to work on yourself. Your attention and energy are like prey. They are what people (hunters) are usually after once you are available to be needed and used. I believe this: ***people are as distractive in your life as much as you are available, and they are alive and awake, ready to take, take and take some more from you.*** But, at 5am, nobody really needs you. Nobody calls you for help. Nobody needs to vent. Nobody needs a shoulder to cry on. Nobody needs a question answered. Nobody needs some help because they can't fix something. At 5am, nobody feels bored and in need of love or attention. But why? Because they are dead to the world at that time. That's when I choose to strike and strive. That is when I am most attentive and alert for myself. That is when I am most successful as a hunter towards my personal goals.

5am Is a Time to Be

One of the justifications for showing up early for me, which at first I shut down, was this: *I will stay in bed for as long as I feel like it, and if I don't have the time to do everything I want to do today, I will just be quicker at doing more stuff when I get up.* And this was my issue. I thought getting up at 5am was only to have more time to get more done. But I was wrong. If you wake up early just to have more time to do more, then you are missing the other half of the point. Waking up at 5am is not just to have more time to **DO** more, but to have more time to **BE** more. You don't wake up at 5am to answer more emails, or make more calls or do the dishes. No, it is simply a time to just be with you. Be more at peace with yourself. Be more calm and meditative. Be more relaxed and stress-free. Be fully present in your own life without interference. It is a meditative time, and even a productive time, but not one of doing, but one of becoming set free from the emotional burden in your life.

Seeds Need Darkness to Grow. 5am Is Your Best Soil

For me personally, 5am is a great soil. At 5am in the morning, I feel like a tiny seed planted for the sole purpose of growing. And so, at that time, I am not pouring anything into anyone but myself. At that time, I water myself with my time and positive messages while I wait for the sunshine to arrive. Many people see the daylight as an indication of growth. So, they wait till it is bright outside before they allow themselves to rise and shine. But growth often starts in the dark, and 5am is usually a dark time of the day to start rising. So, rise like the great seed you are. Let people see you when they wake up and say stuff like this: *you always wake up happy, you always wake up smiling, you always wake up vibrant. You are very lucky all of these going well for you.* Your success begins to seem instant to them. But we both know what was going on below the soil while everyone else was asleep.

5am Is for the Greater Good

Everything we want always demands something from us. To be happy, I had to sacrifice a few things, and not sleeping for longer hours was one of them. If you were like me before, I usually slept for many hours, woke up later during the day, and still felt tired when I woke up. And then I went through the day tired, fed up, sad, angry, frustrated, and so on. But the moment I started waking up earlier than usual, the reward began to outweigh the detrimental loss of the sleeping hours I had before. I sacrificed a few hours so I could have a great positive experience of my day because I would rather wake up tired due to less sleep than go through the whole day well-slept but sad, frustrated, and disappointed about my life.

5am Helps Slows Us Down

It is impossible to enjoy the little moments in life if you are always in a rush to get through them. That was my life before I started waking up at 5am. Often our life is a minefield because we are mindless of it. We take no notice of the little but important things until it's too late. Waking up earlier, however, slows us down in a way that helps us to be more observant and absorbent about the little things that matter. It helps us feel, listen and taste life in a deeper way rather than mindlessly and meaninglessly. Waking up at 5am slows us down in a way so that we are able to see the little parts in our lives that are falling apart, and also the parts we've worked hard for and earned, and by doing so triggers gratitude and contentment. When we are not slowing down, we are doing the opposite: rushing, stressing, missing out. We forget the little important things when we are in a rush.

Moreover, rushing usually indicates worrying. It indicates that we are somehow behind, that we are controlled, that we are under some sort of pressure to be somewhere, and by not being there might be detrimental to our existence. Such a way of life puts unnecessary fear into our minds and blindsides us. And by doing so, we miss out on the little issues in our life that then become bigger problems. We must understand that the heart sees what the eyes miss, and by rushing, the heart fails at this ability too. This usually leads to our relationships suffering, our health suffering and our minds suffering.

Often, constantly being in a rush indicates that we owe our lives to someone else or something bigger and more important than ourselves. And this is among the few reasons as to why we make so many mistakes in lives that we could have avoided making. However, when you wake up early, you have a sense of ample time, and that slows you down to slow things down and, by doing so, you make fewer mistakes because you are not in a rush to be anywhere else.

5am Is Something to Be Proud Of

For me, 5am was an inconvenient time to get up. It was hard, it was unnecessary, and nobody I knew did.

"So, why must I?" I asked myself.

"Because I am not the same as everyone else. Because I have a goal and they don't. And I can't have a goal and stay in bed all day and expect to achieve it."

When I started waking up early, I started having this sense of hope and accomplishment. By just getting up early, I surprised myself. I was gaining more courage that I could indeed achieve anything, no matter how difficult or impossible it may seem. For me, staying up late had become a habit, and to some degree, natural. However, I knew that what was easy wouldn't challenge me, and I needed a challenge to indicate that this time I was really serious about my goal. I realised that it is easier to stay up in the evening than to wake up early. I quickly realised that showing up at a not-so-suitable time can prove that you are very reliable and dependable at an inconvenient time. With this realisation, achievements became easier for me to accomplish.

5am Is a Time of Thinking Manually in an Uninterrupted Moment

The brain functions better when it is fully focused and uninterrupted. This is what makes 5am an ideal time to use our brain for maximum engagement for our benefit. This is what makes thinking manually highly beneficial at 5am (the uninterrupted moment).

We often end up making bad choices and incur problem after problem because our brain is on automatic all the time. Our brain is constantly making choices for us and coming up with hasty automatic decisions to balance out our demanding lifestyle, and we are letting it because it is the easiest way to get through the day. Thinking, on the other hand, takes focus and attention, and we don't have that kind of time, right? This is what makes 5am a special time to get up. If your day usually starts at 9am, now you would have four hours spare to play around with. If it starts at 8am, then now you have three whole hours to play with. Getting up early means you have room to bloom into anything else you might not have had the time for previously.

The idea that the brain should do what it does without guidance is why we are constantly stressed and feel overworked. It is why we often feel lost in life. Yes, the brain does the thinking for us. But, sometimes, it does not help us. Sometimes, the thinking it does isn't what is helpful for our personal growth. It is what we are used to doing that has become an automatic response and now has also become an obstacle to our personal growth. Sometimes, the brain does what the body wants until the brain is made to do otherwise. Sometimes the brain does what our emotion wants. Sometimes the brain does what our desire wants. Sometimes the brain just does what it wants even if it isn't what we should do. Often the brain cannot differentiate between what's morally right to do and what we shouldn't do because it feels right to do at that time.

Thinking manually in a few words is telling the brain what to do! It is a deliberate attempt to use our brains for our gains. It incorporates attention, intention, reflection and a sense of resolution. *But the brain does that for me automatically*, you might say. Yes, it does, but the brain does not tell itself to solve your problems for you. That is on you to command it to think and come up with resolve.

So, yes, you know you have a brain, and you know what it does and how it does what it does. But how often do you use your brain to solve your personal issues in comparison to it using you to get into more problems in life?

We know we need to get up, and yet we think it is okay not to. We know we shouldn't eat too much unhealthy food, and yet we live on junk meals, day in and day out. We know we have a deadline coming up in a few days, and yet, we ignore it because we think we can rush and get it all done after a night out and with a hangover the next day.

Thinking manually is not just being conscious that you have a brain and you know what it does. It is also that you can sit down with it in an attempt to use it purposely to think, strategise, plan and come up with solutions to your problems. And, for that, you need an uninterrupted moment, and that moment is at 5am.

5am Helps Make Changes Around the Unchangeable

I live at a place surrounded by noisy neighbours. One is a teenage boy who screams and swears at his single mum from the moment he wakes up to just before he sleeps. Also, there are two little boys living on the opposite wall of my teenage boy neighbour, both of which enjoy running around the house and making loud noises. Their parent also argues a lot, their father full of rage, swearing loudly and throwing things around the house. I can hear everything from my wall. To top it off, there is a loud group of cohabitations living opposite my house. This meant that from, let's say around 7am, the quietness of the day instantly fades away as the noises start, as the banging starts, as the thumping gets louder and more consistent.

It might have been easier to change my life if I lived somewhere quieter or alone in a desert. It might have been easier to change my life if I could just tell my neighbours not to make any noise all day. It would have been easier to change my life if I could just tell my boss at my workplace to allow me to start two hours later each day instead of at 9am. It would have been easier to change my life if I was able to afford a guru, or a yoga instructor, or a gym right outside my house. It would have been easier to change my life if there were more hours on the clock. It would have been easier to change my life if I lived in a city that had a path for running or jogging. It would have been easier to change my life if the internet didn't exist and social media wasn't around to distract me. It would have been easier to change my health if working out was less challenging, and the takeaway didn't taste so damn good. But guess what? These are things I couldn't change.

All of these unchangeable reasons provided me with the perfect excuse for accepting a life that wasn't making me happy. But at some point, I realised that if I wanted better, I had to accept that I couldn't change these external things. My life could only change if I did first. And it starts with waking up earlier than everyone else, and doing things differently from that moment on. I learned this life-changing logic: **When you can't change** *what is around you, you have to accept it for what it is, and then make some adjustments to adapt to it in a way that allows you to make the positive changes you want to see in your life.*

Waking up earlier than everyone else allows you room to adopt changes that might not be suitable for a later time. It provides room for improvisation and adjustments. It helps you to work your way around things you can't change before the things you can't change get in the way of your intention to change.

5am helps us start our day feeling mentally pampered not hammered

Often we ignore the importance of our mental health care for other life's matter. And I do understand why. We have a boss to impress weekly. We have a family to attend to daily. We have friends that makes us feel less lonely perhaps, and more important that everyone else, maybe. We have a lover that we don't want to think that we are selfish for taking the time out for ourselves. We have a body that needs to look in good shape, a face we love to look pretty and handsome and a body we spend money on to smell pleasantly good daily. We have an Ego that makes us feel superhuman and emotionally unbreakable. But our mental health, our mind, I mean who cares, right? I never did. Not until I started breaking down and then I gave myself no choice but to care. So, ever since then I never accepted having no time as a reason enough to let my life negatively affect my mental health. On a daily basis, I make it important to practice self-care at the crack of dawn. I sit down and I journal. I have a nice shower. Eat a nice breakfast. Listen to a nice music. Put my legs up, etc. Let's use this metaphor for a minute:

When going on a journey, we don't wait till after the journey to check if the car has enough petrol or if it is making the right noise when turned on, right? We check our car before the day's activity. We make sure it is cared for and in good condition. Why? We need it at its best throughout the journey. We don't want it to break down. And here is something to ponder on: *if you take a car to everywhere else everyday but the mechanics, pretty soon it will break down and won't be able to go anywhere, not even to the mechanics.* We are like cars, often we need care. For cars, perhaps the care might be needing to change the oil, windshield cleaning, the tank filling, the inside clearing. Mentally our mind needs similar care to carry on stronger and better throughout the day. But what do we do? Nothing impactful or helpful. We have no time for our mental health, so we compensate by giving it the leftover of our effort at the end of the day. Self-care is not primarily to recover at the end of your day or your week. Self-care majorly benefits our mental health throughout a long day. Self-care first thing in the morning helps you engage with the outside world in a way that eliminate or reduces your stress level for that day. Self-care puts you in a good mood throughout the day. It makes you feel more important and worthy. Self-care is simply the management and maintenance of our mental health throughout that day.

If we take on the approach that we are too busy, if we have a to-do list that caters for everything else but has no room for our mental health care, and if we constantly fail to get up early for our mental health, we are more than likely going to end up staying up all night because of it, worrying, stressing, unable to sleep because our brain is in overload, unprepared for the day and uncared for before that day's busyness commenced.

Have The Go In You

Our achievement is determined not by our level of knowledge but by our consistent level of inspiration to bring ourselves to do something with what we know to do.

I believe that the internet is the best thing to ever happen to us all. Among other things, it gave us the very best gift any generation could ever wish for: It gave us equal access to knowledge. The internet gave us more freedom to access tools for life like never before. This meant that there is no shortage of free answers as information will always be in constant generous flow. It is my humble opinion that information is now as common and available and accessible as oxygen. Information is everywhere and in various editions to support reading preferences: In print, audio, or in digital, all accessible through any device. But yet, the vast majority of us are helpless and hopeless in matters that concern life and living well. We simply can't seem to get unstuck in life, and we struggle endlessly to find true happiness and success. My assumption now follows this logic: knowledge is only half of the solution when it comes to showing up for what matters to us in life. People still find it hard to apply what they know because people can't find what they need (inspiration) in what's available: information.

A few years back, I mentored a guy who wanted to change. He's read so many self-help books and bought himself some home gym equipment. But still, he never made it past day one. One thing became clear to me through our conversation on how to help him achieve a positive change with consistency and total commitment. This became clearer to me: despite the knowledge and the tools we might have at our disposal, we are still bound to be resistant to the positive change we want in life if we lack the accessible mindset that ***when it's time to get up, it's go time.***

So, like many others in his shoes, he knew what he wanted: intention. He knew how to get it: information. What he lacked wasn't enough resources or knowledge to start. What he lacked was a push: inspiration. He couldn't bring himself to get off the couch and show up for what he wanted. Idleness won through his laziness. The drive to deliver was missing. After a thorough heart-to-heart conversation, he understood that he wouldn't grow if he lacked the go in himself to grow. More importantly, he comprehended that inspiration is a major key to staying dedicated, consistent, and focused throughout the process of any achievement in life.

The key point here is this: *I believe that there are tons of books out there with a lot of information on how to tackle personal issues, yet many of us are still at a standstill, confused, unable to see a way out. I believe that knowing better does not mean that you will do better. A lot of people know what to do, and they don't do it. Not because they are forgetful but because they are uninspired to do better with what they now know.* Through the above example, there is no doubt that often our biggest issue in terms of personal change isn't really a deficit in knowledge but in inspiration. And, this is what makes this book so unique in its own right.

Positive Thinking

We are all in a race to survive, persevere and prosper in life. But it is only the early riser and the positive thinkers that have the most advantage over every other racer in life.

It is reasonable to say that negativity is a widespread wound in our modern world today. It is also fair to say that at least one person in our inner circle is suffering from depression. While there are only a few ways to heal this widespread wound, I believe that the art of positive thinking is a much healthier way to help you feel great again, and do great things in life. But, first, what needs to change? What we practice daily: our way of thinking.

Negative outcomes and positive outcomes are both habit-driven behaviours, for as humans what we produce depends on what we practice on a day-to-day basis. And what we practice depends on our current perspective. This is why people who think negatively have more negative outcomes in life than their counterparts. Those who believe that they can do something about anything, do much better than those who doubt their ability to get to the finish line of their goal. This partly explains why positive thinkers have more breakthroughs in life. They do so because positive thinking leads to positive performance, and positive performance leads to positive outcomes.

But why is positive thinking important? You may wish to know. So often, people are unable to be happy because they are suffering from negative thoughts. They are always looking for and at the negative things in life instead of looking through them. They expect the very worst to happen to them instead of hoping that something better can happen for them. And, because, they never stop expecting only negative things to happen to them, they often find themselves plagued by problem after problem. From my experience and observation, negative thinking can be considered as a disease that affects the mind which then goes on to negatively affect how we see the unfolding events in every area of our life. And, to cure this disease of negative thinking, we need an antidote called positive thinking.

Therefore, the simple answer to the above question is this: Positive thinking is important because negative thinking exists. Our existence as humans is based on survival. So, our brain is designed to constantly scan for threats. And when we find them, we develop a tendency to live our life around them while we continue to go looking for more threats so we know who, where, and what to avoid at all costs. This is good news but only limited. It gives us a sense of caution. A sense of control over our fate. It makes us care as being caring about danger equals staying alive. However, as humans, among other things, we are designed to take risks to evolve and not just exist in safety and stay indifferent. So, for this reason, threat avoidance can only help us to get so far in life.

Therefore, the downside to the logic of constantly thinking negative is that constantly identifying threats for the sole purpose of avoiding them puts us in a limiting state of being as often threats are an opportunity to evolve. Threats are often threats because they are unfamiliar not because they are deadly. In fact, not all threats are threats. Almost all threats are there to help us do more than survive: they help us to also thrive, rather than hinder us from survival. Threats are merely the means to surviving rewards that endure throughout human evolution.

How do we apply such threats in our reality? When it comes to our normal day-to-day encounters, we consider things like failure, disappointment, rejection, and so on as threats to our survival. So we avoid them at all costs. We do so at the expense of giving away the opportunity to grow and find true happiness. We settle for what we know we are or have become over what more we can become, even if who we are brings us so much physical, mental, emotional, or spiritual discomfort in life.

It is no doubt that negative thinkers have a worse lifestyle than positive thinkers because negative thinking can affect our entire life if we are careless with how we react when things are not going well for us. Negative thinking, when ignored for too long can affect our way of living, belief system, judgment, outlook, self-esteem, confidence, stress level, feelings, and our general personal, economic, and social potential for growth and greatness.

However, positive thinkers are commonly known to find breakthroughs in all aspects of life. They do so because when faced with challenges, through positive thinking they are capable of weighing the pros of the reward above the cons of the threat in life. They can be relied upon to see the path to light despite the strength of any darkness. Those who think positively understand and appreciate that life has it all: The good, the bad, and the ugly. It can be worse, it can be wonderful. They understand what it means and takes to be human. Positive thinkers understand that as humans, we always find more of what we are looking for. We find more bad stuff when we focus on the negative and better stuff when we focus on the positive stuff in life.

An analogy

A thirsty man pours himself a cup of water, full to the brim, ready to drink. A man with a long jacket over his shoulders knocks into him as he stood up, causing half of the thirsty man's water to spill out, and unto the floor. The thirsty man focuses on what's on the floor, but not what's not, like he's done with everything in his life. Looking down at the spillage, the thirsty man gets mad, angry, and upset. He began to have a meltdown. He felt like he's lost everything within his cup.

The guy who knocks into him apologises. "Let me get you another one sir," he says.

"I don't have time to wait while you queue for another cup of water," came a snappy reply from the thirsty man.

"Okay, sir, I understand. Though at least you've still got some water left inside your cup. And you can drink it comfortably," said the knocker.

"It might as well be a single drop left! It's practically empty! You've knocked it all out!" came an angry exaggerative reply from the thirsty man. "And now, I don't have enough," the thirsty man added, his arms waving everywhere in anger.

"Sorry sir, I wasn't looking when I knocked into you," said the knocker politely.

"Well, maybe you need glasses then!" Exclaimed the thirsty man swiftly and harshly.

"I really do apologise sir, I must have dropped the straw hanging out of my jacket pocket somewhere as someone else knocked into me. And I was merely trying to find it," said the knocker.

"I don't care, Snapped the thirsty man.

"At least it's still half full," came a sympathetic reply from the knocker.

"What! Look at my glass cup, it is now half empty! You've wasted my water!" Said the thirsty man, again in frustration.

"Does it really matter that the glass is now half empty or half full?" Asked the knocker. "I mean, I would trade with you right here, right now. For some people, it can always get worse. You have a cup, you have pretty much 50% of water still left in it, I would say, you have it pretty good. Try having half a glass but no straw," the knocker added.

"What difference does a straw make to a glass of water anyway, if the glass is half empty?" Asked the thirsty man who only sees the negatives in everything in sight.

"A lot more than you can see sir," answered the knocker. The knocker let his jacket fall off his shoulder and unto the floor. "I have no arms sir! So I needed to find the straw I brought here with me. Here, have my water, the knocker gestured towards his half-filled glass with the motion of his chin.

"I apologise," the thirsty man finally said in defeat and shame. "I am sorry, I have had an awful week, and I admit, I overacted. Here, let me help you with your glass of water. I truly can't begin to imagine how hard it must be living without arms," the thirsty man admitted sympathetically.

The moral of this story follows: Be upset if you must, but learn to embrace the fact that life is always going to be filled with mistakes. So, don't let the mistakes that occur in your life control your every day approach to life. Setbacks are inevitable and they can happen at any point or anywhere in life. Disappointments can happen at the best moment in life. Rejection can occur at the time you needed approval the most. Therefore, whatever happens, learn to see the upside in life. Do an inventory of what you've still got if you can't find something to cheer you up. Don't let what you don't have cloud your judgment or sight of what you still have. Be kind to others even if life has been unkind to you. Some people have it worse than others and in most cases worse than you. Some people would rather have what you have, or be who you are. While you are upset that you can't go on a vacation today, or sad that you are unable to afford that luxurious item you saw on your social media feed, some people would kill to have a home to go to, a warm bed to sleep in, a family to come back home to and an income to pay the little essential bills that the life you've got affords you unconsciously and effortlessly. Some people pray daily to get out of jail and have custody of their children. Some pray to have a baby. Some people struggle and hope to have peace, good health, have that one friend they could trust, and so on. So, while you wish for more, and while you are upset about the little you've got, don't hang in there too long. Be grateful that you've got what you've got.

Conclusively, nurturing our minds to engage in a constant state of positive thinking is important because it empowers us by helping us to reprogram our minds to be in a constant state of hope, and solution, regardless of what situation we are in. Thinking positively in a bad situation is not faking happiness or ignoring the facts in your reality but instead, it is facing the facts in your reality, and understanding and acknowledging that you have the power to change the undesired reality that you find yourself in: It simply means that you can see a better outcome despite your current reality.

However, when you think negatively, it limits your way out of the undesired outcome in front of you. When we develop a negative thinking mindset, we feel overpowered by the situation we are in instead of empowered, and it becomes hard to see the bright side of life during a challenging time in life.

It also seems impossible to see the bigger picture of the circumstances we are in because negativity wires us to zoom in on only the bad and how it is affecting us negatively. And once we've zoomed in, everything else zooms out: the purpose, opportunity, gratitude, or better choices. But, life is full of options, if we care to find them. This is why positive thinkers thrive. They see options, advantages, and opportunities where negative thinkers merely zoom in on blaming the world around them for how they feel within themselves. And the way we feel within ourselves affects the way we flourish in life.

Positive thinkers understand that it is much better and more effective to put it on ourselves to change than to blame others for our discomfort. Positive thinkers hold themselves accountable to right the wrong. They get up, show up and find a resolve to end their suffering. Negative thinkers are the opposite. They have this limiting internalised belief system that they have no control over a better change in their life.

While often they don't do it consciously, negative thinkers are preoccupied with the impression that life is unfair and unjust. They mentally isolate themselves in a way that they see themselves as no good or no better than everyone else. They see themselves as destined to only have bad luck while others (positive thinkers) get all the good fortunes in life. Negative thinkers, constantly forget that they are no different from everyone else: *that like everyone else they are indeed the creators of their own life choices, masters of their own matters, and authors of their own outcomes.* They often base their biased assessment of feeling unlucky in life on their own past setbacks, and the people that have let them down. However, the real letdown is themselves because they believe that life has conspired against them rather than assessing the choices they've made so far, and the options they can look into and apply to make a better change.

So, at its core, 5AM is all about building a positive thinking mentality. It is about understanding that to think positively is to carry a mental weapon around with you that enables you to win against your personal, economic, and social problems in life no matter what. Positive thinking does not mean that you will never be sad, fall, or have a breakdown or a meltdown in life. On the contrary, positive thinking is a preparation for when you do have those days, and sometimes it is our preparedness or readiness to be able to access a positive thought that helps in evading a miserable day when they arrive.

In practice, when you are worn out by life, positive thinking helps you find the hole in the needle, so you can fix things right. Therefore those who engage in positive thinking develop the ability to seek out favourable outcomes in a miserable situation. This is what this book is all about.

Growth carries few truths.
Here are many of the worthy ones!

A quick note: What makes this book so rare is its ability to make us conscious and undistracted in every moment of each day, and it does so by reminding us that now matters more than later, that how we think is more important than what we do, that what we have is more important than what we want, and that who we can become now is more important than who we were in the past. I hope you find your way back to this book each time you feel like you are drifting away from living life.

PART 1

I

YOUR NEW DAWN

When the day breaks, the night shatters away.
It is the task of the dawn to drown the dusk.
So is the purpose of the present over the past.
This moment you are in is your dawn,
your awakening.

NEW DAY.
NEW MONTH.
NEW YEAR

A year from now, you will see the result or feel the regret. The outcome is in your hands.

I hope this month you choose progress over comfort. I hope this month you don't get in your own way but get further with your goals. I hope this month you make that decision you have been putting off but know will change your life for the better. I hope this month you put you first and not next or last. I hope this month, you chose peace over people-pleasing for their validation. I hope this month you finally recognise your own strength, stop running away from your problems and start facing your battles. I hope this month you fight for you like you have always been worth it. I hope by the end of this month, you can say *I am better, healthier, wiser, happier and stronger because I didn't turn my back on me again, but instead, I chose to have my own back.*

There is nothing more personal than wanting the best for yourself, going out there and doing it by yourself. Just wow yourself a lot this year! You owe yourself love. You owe yourself pure joy and peace. You owe yourself many proud moments in life. You owe yourself many adventurous stories. You owe yourself rainbows and sunshine. You owe yourself the best version of you. You owe yourself a well-lived life.

Have a year of passion and purpose.

Have a year of winning and learning.

Have a year that ends in flourishes, not just flaws.

Have a year that will end so much rain and pain.

Have a year that will make you smile and shine.

Have a year that you wouldn't want to end.

Have a year that makes you want to want more, do more and be more.

Have a year that would make you be like, what a wonderful year! I can't wait for what's next!

Who says it is too late to start? Who says you are too old to start? Who says your New Year's resolution is set in stone and can't be adjusted, dismissed, or rewritten? Who says your last setback was your final comeback? Who says you must start at the beginning of the year, the middle or the end of it? Start when you are ready, but make sure you do start. And if you have started before and stopped because it got difficult, because you created a goal that exceeded your current means, then do yourself a favour, create a goal that is within your reach, and stretch for that first. Don't abandon what's important because it feels too high to reach right now. Check your list of goals and chase a goal on it. Don't finish another big year with nothing ticked off your resolution list. If you are hungry for better this year, show it in your action, the year has been served to you like a meal on a platter: the year is still warm, the year is still fresh, so chew what you can before the year gets cold again on you. If you can't do the first big thing on your list, do the next big ones or the less big ones after that. Just do something this year.

I hope you continue with your personal development coming into this new month. I hope you keep that commitment you made at the beginning of this year. I hope you don't back down when you are tired. I hope you don't stay down when you get fed up. I hope you don't let your breakdown hold you back when things get rough. I hope you let no excuses get the best of your mind when things don't happen straight away. But most importantly, be proud of you for wanting to do better for you and for not giving up on you. Not many see themselves as strong enough to make that kind of commitment to themselves. So, be proud that you see you for your heart, worth, and your hard work.

Hats off to your old self for bringing you this far. But this year, choose to chase more for yourself. Choose to follow your heart, your happiness, your healing, and your health. You are worth this beautiful path. Fight to achieve it. You know you deserve it.

One of the hardest challenges is to bet on yourself when no one is willing to bet their belief on you. You might be the underdog, you might be underestimated, but I have seen it time after time. The underdog can win. You are that underdog because you can win. If you keep showing up and going hard, you will cause an upset this year. You will ruin the betting odds that are placed against you. Many might look down on you, they might discredit you, they might judge you now, but they will watch themselves lose against you soon enough. Just stay in the fight, and stick to this game plan: ***win by any means necessary.***

The more you hesitate to take the next step with your goal, and the more you doubt yourself this year, you will continue to be your own barrier. You will continue to be a settler of less. But if to have a more fruitful year this year is your goal, you must put your goal in motion and believe in yourself. You must simply stop being the immovable object in your path. And start being the unstoppable force that will break through the obstacles in your way.

The kindest thing you can do for yourself is to stay by you when you are going through the toughest period of your life. So, be kind to yourself. Be there for yourself. Stop being absent from your life. Stop leaving much room for darkness and emptiness within it. Seek the light from whatever fires you up, and light up your heart daily with it. Keep in mind that this year isn't going to be here for this long. Keep in mind that by not doing anything that brings joy and happiness in your life, you are wasting another great opportunity to live a more content life.

This year, learn from my lessons: This year, I am finally learning not to rush my progress. I am finally learning not to compare myself to others if I aim to go further in life. I am finally learning that I don't have to settle on materialistic things so I can show off that I am doing better. I am finally learning that there is no shame in having nothing on show because I am building something much more promising in silence. I am finally learning that pictures made public are instant but personal progress is a process that takes time. I am finally learning that just because two people are reading the same book, it does not mean that they are on the same chapter. I am finally learning that one might be further without understanding, and one might be behind with a better understanding. I am finally learning that being slow on a journey is better than being fast and lost on a path. So, today I urge you to learn to spend more time in your reality than you do on the internet. Stop falling for fakes, filters, and people's fantasies online. Keep your progress real by being careful of how much you use social media as a comparison tool. Not everything you see is a reflection of what it really is. It is easy to fake reality through social media so real people can admire them as real, and it is easier to filter what's real to what people like to see and call it a dream life. Don't fall for it. Even a person with genuine progress on social media isn't for us to compare or copy but for us to be conscious of the fact that we have the capability to also create our own success if and when we choose to. Follow the pace of your own progress.

As this new morning greets you, stop being upset about what you can resolve. The clock has reset for you, so show up like you should while it lasts. Don't be inconsistent with your plans and goals. Resist the urge to stop. Resist the urge to chill. Resist the urge to rest before you've earned it. Time won't wait for you. Time won't sympathise with you. And when time is gone, it only leaves you with regrets.

This year, don't discount yourself. Don't sell yourself short again. Don't just be a person filled with worries and sadness, but one with great self-expectations and an implementable plan. Without something exciting to look forward to, life becomes meaningless, and without a plan, progress becomes a mess of a goal. Let your mission be to push yourself to become more. Stay positive and carry out your plan with passion. Make this year count for you.

A friendly reminder, today is not for your laziness, today is not for your comfort zone, today is not for your breakdown, and today is not for your inactivity. Today is not for you to be unbothered about your problems. Today is a second chance to build a better life for you. Being a good person doesn't qualify you for what you deserve. You get what you give, and you earn only what you put your all into. So, get up and get on with it.

New month. New goals. New fight. New height. Show up like you want it to show up. Don't waste another 28, 30 to 31 days wishing for it. Work for what you deserve. Honour your worth by earning it and be proud you made it happen despite that part of your mind that says, s*leep longer, chill, procrastinate, do it later, one other day off won't matter much.* It all adds up. It all makes a difference. It all plays a major part in how you will find yourself by the end of the year.

I hope you know that this year is your own as much as it is on you. I know you've planned for a few changes this year. So how's that going for you? Here's some sound advice to hold onto: By the end of this year, your resolution list will bring you either resentment or contentment. Regret or result. The outcome depends on what you've done and what you've ignored to do. So, to hell with doing it later. Start now. Go for it. You deserve better.

SHOWING UP

*You only win if you get out of your comfort zone
and show up like you are in a war zone.
So, eyes on your goal. Show up for it.
Focus on it. Fight for it. Finish it off.*

Like they say, no pain, no gain. So, show up even if you are tired, show up even if you are fed up, and show up even if you are frustrated. The payoff will be worth the challenge. Truth is, we've all been there before. Tired but still had to keep going. Some of us are there now, some of us are on our way to that point of exhaustion with no expectations met. But, no matter how challenging it is right now, don't let it deter you from showing up today. When you show up you are one step closer to what you want to show up in your life. But, when you don't, you are backing away from what you deserve.

All achievements require attendance: You have to show up before anything starts showing up for you. And you can't show up anytime or anyhow, or anywhere. You have to show up intentionally, consistently and also punctually. There is a certain punctuality necessary when we have a purpose or a goal to achieve. And when we consistently fail to get up and show up, we compromise our commitment, determination, and hope of one day achieving our goal.

"I wish I had more time. I wish I had a healthier body. I wish I had the brains. I wish I had the mindset. I wish I had the equipment. I wish I had the finance. I wish I had the support. I wish I had the motivation. I wish the weather was better today." I wish. I wish. I wish. All this wishing for things to get better is only washing your opportunity away to make something better happen. Stop wishing. Get up and have a go at it with what you have.

Today shake off that feeling of "it isn't happening for me" and focus on your growth. Be clear about what you must do more of, and be very personal about your progress. By all means, be inspired by others and look up to them as a guideline for setting your own high standards. But what you must avoid is demanding immediate results from yourself by comparing yourself to others.

Showing up every day does more than appearance; it also gives me this feeling of reassurance. That's why when I show up every day, my hope level increases, my motivation level increases, my discipline level increases, and it keeps me grounded in this belief that I am getting better and better and stronger and stronger each day while getting closer and closer to my goal.

Often life is like a fighting sport with problems and goals equivalent to opponents. If you want to win in life, you must get up, show up and fight for it. If you are waiting for someone to encourage you before you step into the ring of success, you are in for a never-ending wait. You see, the fight for success is often an individual activity, and a lonely one at that. No coaches, no friends, no fans. And often, no one is in your corner to tell you what to do or to cheer you up when you get up. It is all on you. You have to tell yourself to show up, to keep up, and when you get knocked down, you have to tell yourself to get up and get back in the fight.

Everyone is tired, everyone is fed up, everyone needs rest, but not everyone is using it as an excuse to be passive, inactive and unproductive. If it is important enough to you, you will get up for it nevertheless. So, if you want to achieve your goal, you have no choice but to show up and give it your all. Remember, hard work always pays off.

I learned that I glow up when I:

Shine through my storm.

Heal my hurt.

Overcome my fears.

Win over my mental war.

Unlock closed doors.

Persevere in adversaries.

SETBACKS

Some goals demand not just the best from you but the brave beast in you to show up.

What do you do when you've done everything right and something still goes wrong?

When all is going well the night before but you wake up in hell the next day? What do you do when you have to face an opponent you never knew was coming for everything you've won within your territory? What do you do when an exciting news becomes a disappointing news? What do you do when the worst-case scenario becomes your reality?

If you are having one of the above days today, I hope this helps: The worst things in life can happen when you are about to experience the best time of your life. I learned that one bad news can mentally put your life's progress on hold. I learned that we don't even have to do bad things for bad things to happen to us. But the most important things I have to tell you are these: There is neither cure nor permanent prevention from having bad days. Sometimes when you are winning, life will catch you by surprise with some bad horrible and painful days. And some days' blows hurt the most because life knows how to throw a power punch, just when you feel comfortable and confident in your smiles and wins. And when that happens I have learned to take a moment to collect myself, so I don't crumble and fall apart. I have learned not to react and rush into an emotional crash, but to take a deep breath and think about what has happened or spend some time figuring it out, and then sleep on it, before I act on it. I have learned that it is natural to feel sad and angry when all hell breaks loose in our lives, but we must simultaneously feel that we can survive and restore ourselves too much better days ahead. I learned that sometimes the days that feel like the worst days in our life are often the right days to make us stronger for the rest of our life. I learned that often things happen to us because they needed to happen for us: to prepare us and help us navigate towards better things in life and also evade something worst in the future. I learned that all bad days come to an end if we don't react but act with careful thoughts and a calm mind.

Don't just stay there because you've hit a wall. Walls don't move. You have to move. Don't just stay down there defeated, and in denial that you are capable. Stand determined. Stand discipline.

Roll up your sleeves, take a deep breath, and drive forward. This is the only move that will help you breakthrough. There is a possibility where there is desire, dedication, and conviction. Say to yourself, I won't give up. I won't give in. I won't go away. I will try one more time. I will give it another shot. I will give it my all. I will get up and try again, and again and again. This is how a breakthrough is born. This is how you end up on the other side of your damn wall.

I learned that in life, often the setback you are experiencing right now is just what you need to transform your life around. I learned that you get the prize of failure, which is the lesson before you get the prize of success: the blessing. Every successful story has a backstory anchored to one or more major setbacks. Every great person, at one stage of their progress has been handed setback by life as an accolade for their attempt. So, own your setback. It is the prize before the prize.

Setback sucks. It does. It sucks because it holds you back. It sucks because it sticks the middle finger in your face while you are down. It sucks because you were doing so well until now, and doing so well made you proud of your progress. But being able to get back up regardless of how sad it made you feel and coming back as if you didn't fall flat on your face is a reminder of how strong you are when you don't quit but keep on putting in the work.

Stop letting your setbacks discourage you from your comeback. It is okay to lack success sometimes. It is okay to hit a wall on your path sometimes. Not every day will go well. Not every adventure will end well. But with that said, failure strengthens our courage. Failure strengthens our resilience. We fail so we can learn to fly higher and stronger when we do fall down on our backs. We fail so we can be made aware that there is a part of us that we can rely on when things don't go as easily as expected. So you see, failure isn't a bad thing. Failure is a useful thing. Have a go at a goal, even if you might fail. Today is another day to face your fears, not to back away from them. Don't let yesterday interfere with today.

Don't bail on you when things get tough. Don't leave yourself down there when life knocks you down. Don't blow out the desire of your heart just because you've failed at reaching your goal. Failure is never a reason to give up a dream. There is no happy ending for those who end the source of hope in their heart when the heat gets hotter. Failure is not an undoable thing. In fact, it's a profitable thing to have. Everyone falls face flat at one point or another, but those who succeed despite it don't grow roots where they don't want to stay forever. They get up, and they ride on. So, pick your bike up, pump your tires with courage, fuel your vision with hope, and climb back with courage. Let no one lie to you that you don't have what it takes to mend and finish what you failed at. Always bet on yourself even if the odds add up like a mountain. You are a mountain bike. You are built to climb to the top and over!

Setbacks are not designed to make us break down and feel bad. They are not designed to make us quit, feel useless or helpless. They are not designed to make us suffer. Setbacks are designed to trigger the potential in us and help us leap into a better version of ourselves. Setbacks are designed to shine a light on the path we are on. To help us identify what turn not to take and what turn leads to our goal. Setbacks are designed to liberate us from our hesitation and hardship.

Don't be in haste in the process of your growth. Don't be mad that the result hasn't arrived yet. The best version of you is cooking right now as we speak and as you work hard at it. I learned that what is built to last is quality, and quality will never be created overnight. Quality demands timing. Quality demands patience. Quality demands saying to yourself, "I'd rather wait to become the best of me than settle for the least of me."

Never abandon your goal because you failed during an attempt. Failure is good news for your flair because failure has the capacity to activate a critical part of your ability that is necessary for your goal. Likewise, failure is an opportunity to experience what else you don't know that is necessary to move forward with your goal. Yes, some mistakes are bigger than others, but often the bigger the mistake, the bigger the manifestation of your goal. When we become scared to move forward after a mistake, we automatically limit ourselves from reaching our intended goal. So, don't let your biggest mistake shrink your courage and confidence. Don't let your biggest mistake be your last attempt at getting to your goal. Mistakes happen so we can make adjustments and make better attempts that will lead to us achieving our goal.

I learned that it is impossible to avoid taking risks, miss out on making mistakes and meet our greatest blessing in life. And when we do make those mistakes, we must maintain a strong positive mind. We all live in our heads, so learn to make the thought within your head a positive place for yourself. No matter how bad you've messed up this time, don't let it be the last time you summon the strength to get back up and believe you have the power to clean things up.

Learn not to falter but to take a deep breath and think straight when faced with a setback. It is on you not to keep looking at your failure as bad luck and start looking at it as a saviour to your future. So, learn to stop using your setbacks to trap yourself in a state of sadness. Instead, use it as a tool to set yourself free. I know it is easier to see the negative during a dark period in life. But if you can step back a minute and look hard at the whole picture of your failure, you will see a brighter future through it and because of it.

When we use our setback as an excuse to stay down and broken, we are simply engaging in self-oppression by restricting the self that can offer more to itself. By so doing, we are stealing away our chance of joy and clearing out our heart's jewellery of hope. Simply put, we are holding our opportunity and potential hostage with fear as a gun to its head. But only we can set ourselves free. And it starts by using setbacks as our getaway ticket to our greatness.

I learned that not every path that we find ourselves in leads directly to our destiny in life. I learned that some paths are bridges that we must go over to get to the main road that holds our destination. Sometimes even when things are going well, they won't lead us to what we want because sometimes things happen not to us, but for us, to redirect us to the right path that leads to where we deserve to be.

I learned that setbacks are vital to harvesting happiness. That setback is not designed to make us victims, break us down or make us feel bad. They are not designed to make us quit, feel useless, or helpless. They are not designed to make us suffer or stay the same, nor are they designed to avert us from our path to better. Setbacks are not designed to make us absent from experiencing our little day-to-day moments of joy. Setbacks, on the other hand, exist in our lives to liberate us from our emotional captivity and physical hardship. Setbacks happen to trigger the potential in us and help us leap into a better version of ourselves. Setbacks occur to shine a light on the path we are on, meant to be on and allow us to be more serious, diligent, and vigilant on the journey of our goal or the life we truly deserve to live.

When things get tough, stay strong and go harder. Adversity and setbacks are nothing but a test of endurance, resistance, and then perseverance. So, never give up. The reward always comes after the storm.

Don't let your setback hold you back. Your progress is not supposed to be straightforward, fast or flawless. Winners do fail. And when they do, they rest, reset, then they rise and come back stronger than ever. But they never ever give up! Are you a winner or not?

What if I give it my all again, and nothing good occurs?

What if this setback means that I am not good enough?

What if I fail again because everyone else is smarter than me?

What if I go for it again and I don't get farther?

What if I give my best and I still don't harvest?

What if I say yes again and I get denied or abandoned?

But what if your next try is the closest one, the only one needed to achieve that yes?

What if someone drops out and there is one spot now available to take?

What if last time, the rejection had nothing to do with you, and it just happened that you were in the right place at the wrong time?

What if you succeed this time around?

You see, I have learned that **what if** is like a coin with two sides, and there is always a possibility to win where there is a **what if**.

Stopping feeling useless just because you failed. Failure doesn't mean you are rubbish or incapable. Failure doesn't mean you need to abandon your courage and beliefs, withdraw your dreams and settle for a lesser life. Failure means there are prospects for you to evolve.

The cure for cowardliness is nothing but setbacks. Only the valiant person who chooses to conquer their fear of living will never have to know what it's like to be a victim over their own life.

II

WEAKPROOF MINDSET

*Hell can't melt a solid mentality.
This is why those whose minds are the strongest
last the longest during the most disruptive
storms of life.*

MENTAL MATURITY

Mental maturity is key to your happiness. Mental maturity is reaching a stage where you become the first priority of attention in your own life.

Maturity is understanding that no matter how sad you are, it is still up to you to show up for your life. To check up on you when no one is asking. To care about your progress even when no one cheers for you. To heal your own wounds when no one hands you a bandage. People owe you nothing. Not gratitude, not respect, not a single sound of their heartbeat, but you, you owe yourself everything you expect from others. So respect your power to manifest anything you want so you don't become a victim of fruitless expectations, frustration and disappointment.

I am at this stage in my life where my unknown limits get me up. I am at this stage in my life where I am unlearning my fear of trying new things. I am at this stage in my life where I am unbothered about people doubting me. I am at this stage in my life where I am unburdened by who has left me. I am at this stage in my life where my peace feels untouchable by anyone not respecting my boundaries.

I am at this stage in my life where I feel unbelievably happier, stronger, wiser, better, by putting myself first. I am at this stage in my life where I have stopped focusing on the many things and started flourishing through the little things in life: sleep, solitude, joy, entertainment, family, fitness, food, and the great company of friends. I have stopped worrying about how many problems I have in my life constantly or how much I should be making and started focusing on how well I can live each day. Neither I nor you will live forever. Our jobs will outlive us. Our possession will outlive us. Our problems will outlive us. The only way to outlive any of them is to live each day as best as we can and as if it is our last day.

Good vibes only today. I am at this stage in my life where only a good vibe is good enough. So if you don't give me a cozy vibe, loyal vibe, check on me vibe, you look great vibe, let's fix it together vibe, I love your boundaries vibe, go smash it vibe, then we can't hang out. We are either wearing matching vibes, or we are clearly not on the same team. I am at this stage in my life where my energy costs more, where my time costs more, where my peace costs more, where my happiness costs more, where my attention costs more. If you have nothing of value to trade for any of them. I can't afford to let you have any of them.

I am at this stage in my life where I am experiencing that happiness happens and last when it is not forced but done by choice. My choice. By choosing to recognise that my heart isn't meant to hurt, hold sadness or resentments alone, but more than anything else, it is also meant to have and hold unto memories and moments of joy and excitement.

I am at a stage in my life where I feel constantly bound by this duty to make me happy. And I think it's a reasonable obligation I must uphold until I can no longer carry this body around that I call my own home.

I am at that point in my life where I am starting to understand that spending every minute of my life around others is unhealthy. That alone time is what heals my soul. And that solitude is not a moment of loneliness but one of gathering oneself together and generating independent happiness from within myself.

At this point in life, I've stopped worrying about the *what ifs*, the *it might not work*, the *what will they say*, the *I am not that lucky*, the *God is not on my side*, the *I am not good enough*, the *what if I am wrong*, the *what if I fail*, the *what am I thinking thinking I deserve this*, the *I don't want to be the odd one out*. This point has created the amazing version of me you see now.

Be mindful of your emotion today. Our emotions can make us become motionless. So, today, be careful not to be held back by your sad emotions. Yes, feel the pain, the hurt, the breakdown, the rejection, the failure, but don't let it consume you. Will it be easy? No. Is it possible to achieve? Yes. Is it necessary to do? Yes. Then it is 100% required. It is really hard to find happiness with a heavy weight of sadness sitting in your heart. Reflect on what's hurting you, then relieve it from your heart. Doing that releases you into a happier state of being.

Stop wishing people would think of you differently. That puts pressure and stress on your mental health. You can't control what people say to you or about you and how they think of you. What you can control is how you present and represent yourself despite their spite and despite what they have to say about you.

I am at that stage in my life where I am diligent with how my day affects my life and how people do too. A stage where nothing that offers me suffering is allowed to survive. I am at this stage in my life where avoidable problems have no space to occupy. A stage where my peace is not an option, but its presence is absolute. I am at this stage of my life where my boundaries are not up for negotiation. I am at this stage in my life where priority is personal, and my mental health comes first. I am at this stage in my life where if any of us is struggling we support one another till it's gone and not cut the chord and hide until it's over. I am at that stage in life, where I won't waste my time on time wasters, naysayers, and haters. I am at this stage in my life where I realised that life is too short to be faking smiles with real people. I am at this stage in my life where if our energy doesn't match, and the flames aren't burning and warming our souls, I will let you go.

POWER MENTALITY

It does no one good to collect valuables when they live in a home with weak walls.
A mind is like a wall. The weaker it is, the more vulnerable it is against the storm that is bound to blow.

I learned to believe that I can manifest all things within my imagination. I learned that we can be in the gutter and also be destined for greatness. I learned that where you are does not define who you can become. But how much you are willing to strengthen your mindset, how far you are willing to stretch your imagination and how much you are willing to give into it day to day to manifest it makes the differences between where you are and who you are and where you can get to and who you get to become. The spotlight today is known to hold those whose history rest on a humbled beginning. Those whose story can be traced back to a past history of struggles. But they had a dream. They made it happen with gut and grit while in their various gutters. They made it happen against all odds. You can too.

Working on yourself isn't going to get easier. Some days it is going to be a struggle. Some days it's going to seem like a hassle. Some days it's going to become your toughest battle. But stay in it. The bad days aren't there to last but to test how much you want it. So, no matter how hard it gets, push harder each day. Remember, motivation is not always going to work. So, learn to push yourself to be mentally disciplined every day. Say yes to every challenge that comes your way, and when you can't find any, create some for yourself. Wake up at 5am even if you don't have a purpose yet. That itself is a purpose. Get up as soon as your alarm sounds, so you can be mentally ready for when things get tougher in life. Expect the bad days to come as you get older.

My first victory of the day is making an alliance with my mind so it is in accordance with my day's goals. It is not an easy fight. It is a fight of my willingness as much as it is a fight of my choice. You see, the mind can be a poisonous opponent or a potent, powerful ally and teammate, depending on how I start my day. Do I wake up and take control, or do I wake up complaining? It's a matter of choice, not circumstance. I can either let my mind tell me lies to defeat me today, or I can tell my mind why I won't step aside today. And to win over my mind, I wake up intending to dominate my mind by being optimistic about myself and my goal and by dodging every doubt my mind throws at me, blocking every discouragement and beating down every fear my mind kicks me with. And then, I submit my mind to my needs. That's how you can fight each day and win against your mind.

When the going gets rough, you don't stop. When the going gets tough, you don't quit. When the going gets you lost, you don't surrender. When the going gets stormy, you don't hide in distraction. When the going gets complicated, you don't look for an easy exit out. When the going gets challenging, you get stronger, you get smarter, you work harder, and you get through.

To anyone who laughs at your struggle, who laughs at your search for inner peace, who expects you not to show up with a smile. Silence then by showing up. Silence them with your smile. Silence then with your strength. Silence then with your shine. Silence them with your consistency. Silence then with your success. Tough people are the people who control their upset, talk less, heal as they struggle, take more actions and have the last laugh through their breakthroughs.

Don't be upset because someone sees you glowing and calls it luck. Be proud of yourself. Be happy, and applaud yourself that you've made something that seems impossible to others look like instant magic to them. Nobody usually sees the challenges we had to conquer. Nobody usually sees the work we had to put in. Nobody usually sees the tiredness in our eyes, in our demeanour. All they see is the result. All they see is some assumptive fortune or coincidence. But you know it wasn't by accident. You know it wasn't through some unexplainable fortune. It was because you put yourself first, and you witnessed it all first-hand. Be proud of who you've become. Be proud of how far you've come. Be proud of being there to see it all, to experience how hard you've fought against your mind. How much you've given into it to earn what people now call luck, coincidence, cheat code. Be proud of you.

I have learned that some mindsets are not designed to help you win big in life. So, I have learned to adopt the lion's mindset to cut my losses and win in life. I have learned that lions can't eat until they've shown up to hunt. I have learned that lions don't stop even when hurt. I have learned that lions don't run around all day wasting their energy. I have learned that lions don't hang around the wrong crowd. I have learned that lions stay patient during their hunt. I have learned that through early setbacks a lion learns to isolate its goal from the herd (distractions) and stay focused on one prey (goal) at a time. I have learned that lions might be natural hunters (talented) but they are not experts (wise) from birth. I have learned that lions act without hesitation and they win at the end of the day because they display their lion's mindset.

Whenever quitting plays out in my mind, I think of the payoffs. I think of the pain I have been through. I think of where I don't want to be. I think of my happiness. I think of my value. I think of my energy. I think of my worth. I think of my legacy. I simply think today is not going to be the day to stop me. I am seeing this through. So, think about your why before quitting gets the best of you.

I won't fall for the easy way out again today. I am fed up with this less, of this stress, of all these messes in my life that makes me feel helpless. And now, it's my showtime. So, if I have to get up for it early, if I have to fight for it early, if I have to learn all about it early, if I have to plan for it early, if I have to earn it this way, if I have to work very hard for it this time, then so be it.

Don't leave your mind out of the equation of your progress. Your body can't fight and win against the strong invisible enemies in your mind. Likewise, don't neglect your body. Your mind needs a strong castle to rest in when the external storms blow too strongly.

I am proud of myself today because I have had my back for so long. I have always had to fight for what I want. I have always had to wear my heart on my sleeves. I have always had to stand up for myself. I have always had to earn it the hard way. The callous way. The falling and getting back up way. And I respect myself for it. I always will. (I am a survivor.)

I realised that there is fear in everyone. That the fear in each one of us is only as loud as we let it be. But when we take care of our minds and clear the doubts within, when we push ourselves to achieve something and make ourselves proud, the voice of fear gives up and stops speaking to us.

When we postpone the idea that our idea isn't good enough, that our vision isn't possible when we say just one more try, that idea eventually becomes a reality. So, are you willing to believe in your vision until further notice? Are you willing to be committed until further notice? Are you willing to get up early until further notice? Are you willing to get to your destination until further notice?

You think your comfort zone is your friend? You think your comfort zone has got the same goals as you? You think your comfort zone wants the best for you? No, not one bit. Your comfort zone is a false friend. Your comfort zone loves that you've settled for a mediocre life. That you are on the couch, hating your body, your mind, your life. Hoping to catch some sleep before you go to that stressful job tomorrow. Your comfort zone is your biggest enemy in the life you wish to have but don't have. If you want that life that would make you happy, you need to part ways with being comfortable.

They say no pain, no gain. But remember this today, it is not only the pain that makes us progress, it is also having a plan. It is almost impossible to maintain progress without a plan. But when you have a plan, it becomes easier to hit your goals. Plans help us measure the distance between what we have to do, what we do and what we've done. A plan turns your pain into purpose. So don't suffer pointlessly. No plan, only pain, brings no gain. So, make a plan before you face the pain. That's how you benefit from pain.

Even though the outcome is beneficial to my happiness, I have learned that not all progress is fun or enjoyable. I don't have to love doing the work, I don't have to like sleeping less because of it, but if I can't live better without a goal, then I must learn to live with doing what it takes to achieve it.

RESILIENCE

Resilience is the ability to be able to endure where others might end their venture to persevere. Resilience is not just about saying no; it is also about saying yes in a situation where it would have been easier to say no.

Today I hope you start climbing back up. I hope you give up, not on yourself but on the idea that rock bottom is all that you can offer to yourself. Pick yourself up from where you've let yourself go. You've fallen so far down, and? Okay. But you don't have to drown in a mental state of helplessness, nor should you bow down to defeat. Everyone falls off at some point in life, but those who really do want better in life never settle for rock bottom. They don't lie there and claim defeat as their final destination. They don't hit the ground and build a shelter there and call it their home. They help themselves back up, and they start climbing out of the hole they've found themselves in. So, today, I urge you to give yourself a nudge, a push, a pull, whatever gets you up, and start climbing back up.

Keep your progress personal. Who is doing better than you is none of your business. Don't stop going just because you can't see yourself growing. You are growing alright. Seeds do grow beneath the soil before they go on show. So relax and focus on your phase. Keep your eyes on your destination and choose your own pace. Run as fast as you can, not as fast as you see others running. Be patient with yourself and keep it personal. Stop letting the idea of instant results interfere with the consistency of your progress.

Don't let your moment of disappointment stop you from your experiencing your excellence. Stay mentally strong. Nothing can beat a mind that isn't afraid to give it all it's got again. Nothing, absolutely nothing, can defeat a mind that isn't afraid to fall and get back right up and say, *"Let's go again, shall we?"* Defeat, you see, is not a destination. It does not mean that you are over. Defeat is an opportunity to come back wiser and stronger than the version which once fell.

When you are broken down in life, and you can't see a way out, learn to lean on what's within: your heart. Lean on how it keeps beating, on how it keeps going, on how it keeps jumping and pumping with life, on how it chooses to keep doing its part. That's how you come out on top.

The best things in life take time. Don't let your haste ruin your chance of happiness. Don't quit too soon. Who knows, the next day might be your big day. So . . .

Dare yourself to keep going when things get tough. Dare to keep going when nothing shows up.

Life is a process, not an instant oatmeal. Don't be frustrated, and don't be disappointed when things aren't going well. Just keep telling yourself that delay doesn't mean denial. Because that's right!

Don't you dare quit because of your struggles. Every battle can be won, and you have what it takes. Struggles are just battles, and you are a warrior of victory. So, buckle up and drive through by all means necessary.

Everyday day, you must get up on your feet and fight to win against life. And when life knocks you down, get back up. When life knocks you against the rope, bounce back and balance yourself. No matter how tired you are, keep coming at life, keep throwing, and keep thriving.

You are still in the fight for as long as you get back up on your feet.

Don't let the end goal rush you. Don't let the end goal overwhelm you. Burnout isn't the way to measure progress. Burnout is how we crash. Work hard but don't overwhelm yourself. How far you can go also depends on when you begin. So let your starting point lead your pace. Progress is not a race. Progress is not a completion. Progress is about realising where you are and making a plan to take you further step by step, day by day.

At first, nobody will believe in you, but their negative opinion about you. They will call you crazy and lost, foolish and a failure. But do not be discouraged. It is only a matter of time before you break through and silence them all. The sweetest victory is proving everyone that doubted you wrong.

Don't stop reaching for your goals just because you feel like your age has reached the end of its opportunity or just because you've wasted the past years away. You are never out of time for as long as you can still take another breath. Press the start button and let the direction of your goal be your race track. Start where ever you are now, even if life feels dark and you are nowhere near where you know comfort. Start even if the vision looks unclear. The beginning of success is never easy, but the end is always worth the hard work.

Never regret going for something you want in life. No successful person escaped being knocked down by life on their way to making a living for themselves. Never give up on where your heart beats to be. That greatness you seek is within your reach, and you are no exception to it. No more excuses, only results. Let today be your beginning and your reality redemption.

Winners don't wait for a lucky day. Winners don't wait for support. Winners don't sit and hope all day long. Winners don't shy away from any challenge. To winners, easy is for the lazy. Easy is for the uncommitted. Easy is for the *I don't want to work for it, but I would like to have it* people. Winners show up for a fight. They show up to earn what they want because they are damn sure they are worth the effort.

Stop letting your mind tell you that you are too tired, too weak, too comfortable to make a positive change in your life. The consequence is always worse than the discomfort of getting up, showing up and doing what you have to do to achieve your goal. So, Get up and get to it.

Never ever give up on what you want to show up for you. I was doubted. I was denied. I was rejected. I was overworked. I was unfavored. I was underrated. I was laughed at. But it became all irrelevant because I never gave up on myself.

Nobody sees the hard work. Nobody sees the commitment. Nobody sees the late nights and the early mornings. Nobody sees the persistence. All they see is the success. Not the daily grind. Not the self-belief. Not the self-learning. Not the self-sacrifices, and not the self-discipline. All of which made it happen. Now you know, it isn't luck. It isn't genetics. It isn't magic. It is down to the character and work ethic I bring upon myself before the world wakes up.

III

HEALTHY TALK

The cost of restoration or reparation is often more expensive than the cost of prevention or progression. So, for those who think working out is hard to stay healthy: Some of us had to learn about staying healthy the hard way. I hope you don't have to. It isn't pretty. It isn't pennies. It is painful. Dreadful. Regretful. So, buy daily into living a healthy life so you don't have to pay hell's bill for an illness that you could have avoided.

LEARNING HOW TO WELLNESS

*The compass to wellness is awareness.
Awareness that your health needs you more than anyone. That your body needs you more.
That your mind needs you more.
That your soul needs you more.*

I learned that healing starts with putting yourself first and doing your best to love yourself. So, stop being upset that no one is there for you when you need them. **Some days you have to be the first one on call. On other days you could be the only one available to call.** Be ready to be the one on the other end reaching out to support you. Perhaps that's what the people you need are also doing to heal too right now.

I learned that wellness begins with facing the mess in your mind and not looking for space in anyone's heart. Everyone else is also trying to cope, so their mind is also occupied. **There is really no peace nor happiness for those who depart their own mind.** So, stop trying to escape your mind. Stop being emotionally homeless, hoping to find a better home in others. Go back to face your mind, figure things out and clear out the mess in it.

If you are feeling stressed out, overwhelmed, anxious, overworked or emotionally crippled today, then do this one thing: **STOP**. Stop that spinning wheel of everything you think you must do and accept this very moment you are in as your stop sign. Now, go on, take it slow, do things at a conscious flow. Do what gives you meaning, do what gives you a good feeling, do what takes away your worries, and do what gives you healing.

I have learned not to dismiss, refuse or resist my help. I have learned that battles persist because those battles are mine to be fought and won. **There is some hurt that no one else is strong enough to heal.** We know those kinds of hurt, and we can only heal those kinds of hurt by putting ourselves in charge of our pain, pushing ourselves in ways no one would, and praising ourselves when no one sees how hard we are fighting every day not to give up, but to stay strong.

A wonderful way to harness wellness is to be grateful for what you have rather than being sad for not having all you want. Stop focusing on what you lack. Stop pouring your feelings into what is missing in your life. **What you have is what is real.** What you have is what keeps you happy. What is missing will always limit how happy you can be if that is all you care about. So be careful not to be carried away by what you don't have at the expense of what you do have.

You are where you are right now because that's where you need to be to say, *"I don't deserve this. I deserve better. I want to do better. I want something better than this."* So, stop waiting to be in a better position before you change what you are unhappy about yourself or your life. That is a hopeless and endless wait. **Building yourself into better takes falling down, breaking down, burning out, being at your lowest period and darkest point in life.** If that's where you find yourself right now, congratulations, you are at the right starting line. Now, let's begin your personal growth.

The weight of not being myself was lifted once I learned that nobody is perfect, but everyone is unique. So, I stopped trying to be perfect for anyone. I stopped trying to hide my flaws so others might find me faultless. *I stopped trying to impress anyone who wasn't happy with the real*

me. If you want to be happy in life, be the real you, embrace it, accept it, and express it. Perfection is a stage of fakery. An illusion that drives us away from what makes each and everyone one of us special. You are special, that's the real version that matters, and it is indeed better than an illusion of perfection.

Healing starts by learning to reveal and not conceal what you don't like to yourself and the people around you. Fixing what you must and letting others understand what they do and how what they do to you hurts you. Showing them you care about yourself just as much as you care about them.

In each one of us, there's a source of light that no force of nature can destroy. It comes from the depth of your caring, kind heart. Let that source power you. Let it light you up. **Let that light in you shine bright like it is meant to.** But don't just let it flow within. Let it out of you by expressing the joy in you. Let that light illuminate the world around you and beyond.

I learned that I don't always have to be productive to have a sense of happiness. Sometimes what I need to be happy is not by doing something but by feeling something: peace, calm, rested, unrushed, stress-free, worry less, and recharged. And this I can only achieve by saying to myself, "Do nothing today, put your feet up, and have a good meal. Pour yourself a nice drink. Let the four walls that hold everything else out be soaked in a piece of relaxing music. Watch a film or a show and have a nap in-between."

I have learned that our toughest battles can never be won through comfort but through effort. *I have learned that we have to make our life our fight, and challenge ourselves to step up for ourselves.* I have learned that the heaviest, roughest, or darkest days are the ones that help us discover we are the strongest and kindest person we will ever know and have.

I learned that healing is not just based on what you start doing differently but also on what you stop doing currently. Like, stop dealing with bad energy around you. Like, stop begging anyone to stay who doesn't want to. Like, stop trying to impress people who exploit your strength but give you nothing in return. Like, stop fighting for something that constantly shows resistance to your worth, care, love, time, and energy.

I learned that we hurt for a reason. That our hurt is not a reason to stop growing, but a phase, a necessary season. I learned that hurt happens to test our strength, and healing comes next after to make us aware that we are made of unlimited strength to regenerate our healing again. So, don't be discouraged when you fall behind on your healing and begin to hurt again. Just stay determined to heal again.

Healing seasons come and go, so do well not to miss yours. Don't hold unto the memory of hurt as if you aren't capable of healing again. Healing again is never easy but nevertheless a necessity for your progress in wellness. Truth is, we find happiness, then we hurt, then we heal, then we hurt once more just to heal again. You see, sometimes healing is hard because the hurt came from a period that once held us together. Like sweet apples, so can a sweet moment in time become a bitter memory with time. Happiness ripens, then rotten, with time. You can bloom one season and then dry out the next. You can bear ripe apples one season, then see them rotten and fall the next. But you are still that same tree that has seen many changes in a lifetime. You are capable of newness, capable of wellness, capable of blooming through this new season you find yourself in. So, believe you will heal again.

I am happy to have cracks in my life. They give me light, and they help me breathe. I wish never to be perfect, never to be complete or concealed. Perfection can leave no room to add anything. I don't want to live a boring life of not having anything else to discover about myself. And sometimes, having some air come in through the cracks is just what we need to realise that, we are still human, that we can carry on just fine by being ourselves and to ensure that we don't hold ourselves to an unreasonable high standard and suffocate.

Today, I hope you get there soon too; to a happy place, to a peaceful place, to a place as colourful as a fresh rose, and as calm as a tall tree. I hope you get to a place that decorates your face with more smiles, more joy, more adventure, and more rarity of genuine, kind people. Today, I hope you realise that such a place is for people like you: kind, helpful and loving.

Stop feeling sorry or lost today. In fact, be grateful to be. Wellness usually starts in a difficult mess. Often the difficulty is difficult because it is unfamiliar, not because we are incapable. Live for the newness, and pay attention with boldness. Learn about the new things you are experiencing right now. Let whatever you are going through lead you forward. Love wherever it is taking you through. You are not lost. You are at a point in your life that isn't familiar. You are simply loading into your next stage in life. This period of your life is the next stage in your self-discovery journey. Be happy, be proud, be excited and don't give up on what else there is to your being.

You don't have to tolerate people's negative energy just to be respectful or accepted by them. People's approval is worth less than your peace of being. Negative encounters only cause damage to our emotions if we keep allowing them to persist. If you wish to be mentally healthy, don't let anyone destroy your joy today. Let nobody have the better of your feelings. That is often their way of paralysing your soul's glow and controlling your progress in life. Choose to be in charge of how happy and peaceful you want to feel today.

If you wish to have and sustain wellness, cut ties with those who wouldn't come to your aid if you were in a critical condition today. Keep the people who would turn up when you are in need of a chat, a hug, a meal, or advice. Stop wasting your time on people who never have or make time for you. They don't care about you. Imagine, if they don't have time for you while you are alive, what makes you think they will attend your funeral when you are dead?

Wellness is also accepting yourself in your own skin and being unapologetic about your positive energy. In other words, be who you are, even if who you are is the one people call a weirdo. Express it as it is. Don't fade into commonality just to avoid being called out as weird. Some people will call you weird for being happy, for smiling without fail. But what they meant is that you are a rare kind. That despite the world consumed by unkindness, you are kind without expectancy and with consistency. And that is strange, weird and unusual. So, take it as a compliment.

Believe it or not, you are the strongest person you will ever have around you. So, be kind to yourself. Surviving each day isn't a walk in the park. Be proud of yourself. And applaud yourself as often as you wake. You've earned it for not quitting. For holding on, on those days you barely could. For tolerating people that never deserved your presence.

Today, be a giver to yourself. Be kind to yourself. Enjoy your own energy. Enjoy your own light. Enjoy your own love. Enjoy your own company. Enjoy your own joy.

Take some time off when you feel off. Your health is more important than anything else. Don't be reckless with your health. Be smart enough to sit things out if you don't feel well. Your job can wait because it won't wait for you if your health becomes a problem or gets worse. Take care of yourself because when push comes to shove, you are on your own, and you are all you've got.

Today I choose to handle myself without criticism but with care, with curiosity, and with confidence.

Those who condemn your essence, to hell with them. Who needs others' validation when you are born with a voice of your own. Not you! You matter, okay! Look at yourself in the mirror and repeat that to yourself daily. Stop wasting your feelings on being upset, on feeling useless or unloved. Strip away that sense of not being good enough or not having enough. Your flaws don't make you any less unique. Neither does not having everything make you any less adequate.

There is healing in just putting your headphones on and spending that quality time with your mind in reflection. By doing that, you are accessing so much the outside world can't provide. Through my journey of self-discovery, I uncovered that there is so much to discover, admire, find, receive, and release from the quiet engagement with my mind. In other words, your mind holds infinite ways to heal you.

Becoming is an infinite state of being. It is an extension without limitation and, I dare to say it, even an obsession. And there is nothing wrong with being obsessed about what more you can become. Nothing is more magical than becoming the best version of who many said you couldn't be, time after time. It is always a powerful way to empower you to top it up even more!

Feel lost? Write. Feel lonely? Write. Feel hopeless? Write. Feel demotivated? Write. Feel in doubt? Write. Feel anxious? Write. Feel distracted? Write. I write because it brings clarity, for I discovered that clarity brings light on the path of what I want and where to find it. When you have clarity, everything else around what you wish for fades into the darkness. What's left in sight will pull you into its world and be manifested through you.

So often, you must pause to give yourself a round of applause. Believe me, I know. It takes an unseen strength to fight those unseen battles of yours. So be proud of yourself. Only you know in-depth what it took to survive yesterday and be a partaker today.

I learned that holding grudges against anyone is a self-sabotaging emotion. I have learned to stop wasting my rage on people who don't deserve my energy. I have learned that rage is a great source of power. It can bring down mighty forces. So, to you who are mad, angry, upset, raging about your life or anyone in it, use your rage wisely. Invest it into your liberation. Use it to break down the cage that has stopped you from escaping the memories that are holding you back from healing. Turn your rage towards self-empowerment and experience the better life you deserve.

Sometimes I have to remind myself to wake the smile on my face and take things slow in my growth. Progress is not a race. It is a case-by-case situation. The staircase is the same length for everyone trying to rise and grow into a better person. We all get to start from the bottom and not from where we can see those who are already ahead in progress.

Healing starts with awareness. Healing starts with self-worth. Healing starts with courage. Be careful how you stigmatise yourself as a victim of your past. We are made stronger through the pain we've been through so we can defeat the worst that is waiting for us ahead. So, not everything that has happened to you is designed to work against you. Most things happen to work for you. To help you become wiser. To help you become stronger. To help you become bolder for the challenges ahead.

Sometimes the people we love the most are the ones that hurt us the most. But as much as we love them, we must have that tough love conversation with them so they know where we stand and where we are hurting, why we are hurting and who the root cause is. You see, understanding is usually the first step to awareness and resolve. Now that gives them an opportunity to rectify any wrongdoing. And when they don't, you have a difficult choice to make. But, do well to remember this: *a difficult choice is usually the right choice to make. When you stop dealing with certain people, you start healing, and you start winning.*

Let your soul be:

Stress-free daily

Overflowing with brightness daily

Uplifted with pleasure daily

Loved daily

Sometimes we lack the happiness we seek even when we have too much because what we need isn't a thing or a person. Sometimes what you need is not something but somewhere: *a place that isn't toxic, a new environment, a new job, a new beginning, a fresh start, a new day, something that provides you with a clean slate.*

Don't forget that you matter. Don't forget that your energy is for you also. Don't forget that your life needs you too. Don't forget that you are still learning and still figuring life out as you grow and age. Don't forget that your mistakes are lessons to evolve you. Don't forget that your broken heart is still the strongest part of you. Don't forget to understand your mind is your greatest power. Don't forget to love your body as much as you love your phone. Don't forget that you can't make everyone happy. Don't forget that if you work hard enough, you can have what you want. Don't forget that you are unique and valuable. Remember, time might be on your side, but time is equity. You have no ownership to it. Therefore, time isn't yours forever to keep, so make the most of it today. Don't forget any of these. Please.

Be mindful. Comparison can be a hindrance to your success. When we compare our growth to the success of others, hoping to find ourselves at their finishing line, we won't think we are making any progress. And this is the downfall of those who quit after a while. Those who aim to arrive successful do well to remember this: *success is the product of progress. You are doing better than those unbothered about what's bothering them in life. Just remind yourself that you are right on track because you are.*

From my experience, I learned there is a difference between endurance and acceptance in times of life crisis. Endurance keeps us going till we get through what we are going through. Endurance helps us handle what life throws at us. But we must be careful not to make a home in our storm just because we survive. That is acceptance. We must see that we persevere out of such a way of living if we ever want to be fully happy.

To be free and happy in the future, you must know your mistakes before anyone uses them against you. And correct them so no one can define you by them. Unfortunately, some people have a way of reminding you of who you used to be, to bring you back to that victim mentality so they can control you as they see fit.

Stop wasting your life daydreaming about a life that isn't yet in existence. Today is the future you once looked forward to and now get to experience. So live it whole. You see, the future is not measured by distance but by existence. And every second, every minute that turns into hours is your future. Instead of looking forward to the future, look forward to how this next minute of your life can be meaningful to your experience of life.

FITNESS

Chilling never makes anyone rich or healthier, happier or stronger. Get off that couch and workout!

I love my fitness days, the showing up, the working out, the sweat, the gains, all of it. With each exercise, I grin. When my arms hurt, I grin. When my chest beats fast, I grin. When my legs shake, I grin. When my throat burns with air, I grin. When my brain comes to life, I grin. Each push, each pull, each pleasure and each pain screams at me, "Keep going, keep growing. You are a mighty beast!"

The bond between your body and mind is inseparable. So don't just focus on the mind, help your body too. Be physically passionate about what more you can be. Exercise, work out and experience your true strength. Let your fitness journey become a success story that can inspire others struggling with their body and mind.

If you like what you see, don't just wish for it, don't just wait for it to happen. Make it happen. Start working today on what you might wish to have manifested instantly in your life tomorrow. Physical progress always differs for everyone because such progress is a tailored experience that takes account of who you are, how committed you've been, how consistent you've been, and when you started your goal.

Today, make fitness a priority. Plan for it. Your body is the vehicle designed to take your imagination to where it wants to go in your reality. But it can't bring you there with so much unnecessary weight piled on it. So work out, get fit and stay fit. Your success also depends on your fitness.

Let your body be a testament to your ability to write any happy-ending story of your choosing.

For me, fitness is not just about the looks. Fitness is about clearing the mess in my mind. About the quiet peace I get. It is about watching me beat my previous limits. Learning more about my body. Learning more about my mind. Hearing my heartbeat, hearing myself say the words ***just one more, you can do it.*** It is simply pushing myself to create something of myself to be proud of.

Fitness is a daily essential to my life because it gives me calmness. It gives me strength. It helps me concentrate and makes me content. It brings me comfort. It keeps me in control of my body. It gives me a reason to compliment myself and be proud of my decision. It is now your time to choose fitness over laziness.

Your fitness journey is not a competition or a race against anyone but yourself. So, go at your own pace. Lift only what your strength allows. Run only as fast as far as your body allows you. Grow as you go, handle the level of difficulty you can handle and top it up when it gets too easy. Your health journey doesn't have to be identical to anyone else. Just make your health personal and critical to you.

A lot of people see fitness as an escape route or an activity to achieve an impressive body. But I have learned that fitness is not just designed for physical transformation. It is not just an escaping activity. It is a stand-off battle between the negative voice in your mind and the transformative power of your mind to silence them, at your will. Fitness does not just distract you or disrupt your old habits. It distances you completely from your old self.

Working out to have a great body is a great achievement. But having a strong mind and feeling healthy in the process is an unmatched amazing feeling.

It is vital to create time for your health. Don't take good health for granted. Its lack eventually catches up to you. Among many plans of the day, fitness is paramount. It is nearly impossible to enjoy your life while dealing with health conditions. So like it or not, You need to work on your health to have a happy life.

One of the best ways to experience progress in your life is through fitness. Fitness is a form of control, and control is vital to happiness. If you want to be happy, you have to be in control of how you feel. And you can't feel unhealthy and feel happy in life.

I work out not just to build a healthy body. I work out to build a healthy shelter for my soul.

Call it obsession, addiction, ambitious. I call fitness the self hero's duty: a conscious awareness of my ability to save my life and prevent me from suffering physically, mentally, emotionally even spiritually. And that is a serious matter.

Without a little workout to start my day, my body feels tortured, not pleasured. So I get up, put on that music and let my hands and feet make me happy. So, it's growth time baby! Stop chilling. Get up and get chiselled! Let go!!

Even when I don't want to, I still make an effort to get up and exercise because I'd rather my life be more comfortable than my couch.

Spend some time daily with your body. Even if you feel young, strong, and healthy. Treat your body with as much love and care. Nurture it with nature's presence. Gift it the gift of fitness and rest. For, if you take your body for granted today, if you fail to love it and care for it, if you feed it with what's unhealthy for too long, and forsake its cry for help for too long, one day will come, your body will forsake you back when you need it to support you back when you age.

With each year that goes by, we decay physically. Arguably you can get through life without running or lifting weights. But your fitness in health can nevertheless affect the enjoyment of your journey in life. So, today, invest in your health so you can preserve YOU throughout your life.

Don't make the gym the only place you feel comfortable to look after your health. Make your home a health equipped environment. Work out at home whenever you want. Exercise your mind whenever you feel like the alternative use of your time will be wasted on pointless, non beneficial procrastination. Working out only when you go to the gym is like having a house, paying monthly for it and still renting a hotel to sleep in weekly.

Nothing shows up until we show up. So I showed up for another workout today because I love looking in great shape. And I feel great too. This good health, you see, some call it luck. I call it hard work. Because that's what it is.

It hasn't been easy showing up daily for my body. It hasn't been easy getting up when all I want to do is stay longer in bed. But it has pleased me to know that I am committed to seeing the best version of my body every other day.

You can't isolate your health from your happiness. Your physical health is just as critical to your happiness as your net worth or your self-worth.

Another reason I work out is that I don't want to let my body become an abandoned house. I don't want it to deteriorate due to neglect. This body I own is my home. This body shelters the heart that beats for the people I love and the beautiful memories that decorate it. And I must make it homely for all its inhabitants.

MOVING ON/ LETTING GO

We are expected to hold on for others, but to let go, that's for ourselves. So, when you are ready to put yourself first, when you are ready to be fruitful, be like a tree. A tree enjoys the blessing of life after the end of a great season because it understands that there is a purpose in letting go of old leaves.

Personal progress isn't always a kind or noble process. Such growth can often involve making tough choices and emotionless decisions. It can mean losing some loved parts of you by being ruthless in order to be fruitful again. So, stop stressing out about putting yourself first. Stop feeling guilty about cutting off people who held you back. There is progress in letting go. There is peace in letting go. There is freedom in letting go. The benefit does outweigh the discomforting feeling.

There is magic in letting go.

Letting go brings you healing.

Letting go brings you hope.

Letting go unburdens your heart.

Letting go clears your tears.

Letting go pours peace into you.

Letting go clears your path to victory

Letting go gives you a sense of self-respect.

Sometimes letting go is the only way to win. So, if the price for happiness is heartbreak, we must pay it. If the price for peace is being alone, we must pay it. If the price for health is discipline, we must pay it. If the price for wisdom is learning, we must pay it. What makes us grow can be costly, but it is always worth it.

I learned that often our happiness demands radical measures. I learned that letting go can be a good thing. I learned that people aren't permanent. They are constant. They come and go. They stay and abstain. Sometimes they change for the better. Sometimes they leave for the best. And I have learned to live with this fact because I now know the difference between those whose change becomes a light and those whose change becomes a burden. I have learned to know when to hold on tight to them and when to do without their presence anymore. I hope you have the courage to do the same too.

Everything in life happens in turns. We must learn to understand it, and we must learn to recognise the timing of when to let go of the old so we can be reborn with greatness. You see, we can't hold onto hurt and heal at the same time. You have to let go of what happened to you in your old season in order to bloom through the magic of your new season. Be okay to wish farewell to the dead leaves in your life. Let the wind sweep them away from you. I promise you, when you let go, you won't be void of colour for too long.

Don't let looking back hold you from moving forward because if you do, you might open healed scars. Likewise, stop putting yourself in a position to heal from a pain you once prayed to go away. Not every past must be fixed. So, let things be. Move on and look forward to new experiences. Whatever has happened, even if it is something you regret, let it be. Don't try to recreate it just to make it better. Some experiences are a one-time lesson that happened to help us know what not to do ever again rather than what to do better again. Understand that the adventure of happiness always lies ahead, not in the past. So, let the lessons of your past be enough evidence that the past should be left behind.

Sometimes we don't need to be put back together. Sometimes we feel destroyed because we need a total transformation. New blocks. New design. New environment. New surroundings. New outlook in life. You see, sometimes we fall apart not to be put together but to rebuild ourselves from scratch.

So, let go of who you used to be. Let that person stay lost. Let that person be free to fly away to make room for a new you.

There is so much solace in letting go. So today, let go of validations. Let go of permission. Let go of impressing anyone. Let go of feeling useful, needed or the favourite. Instead, choose to please you for a change. Stop being a people pleaser while you continue to live an unpleasant lifestyle. Don't just exist as an *I need to make everyone happy* kind of person. Stop putting too much pressure on yourself to meet everyone's expectations. Give yourself some space and only do what also allows a great amount of your time to be invested in you. You won't live forever, so whatever you do now with your life, be the centre of attention in it.

I: YOU

We all go through the same storms in life. It is how we come out of it or whether we come out of it that makes the difference. It is the choices we make and the way we partake that makes the real difference between me and you.

It is not a coincidence that brought you here today. It is not luck that brought you here today. It is your decision. Where you are right now is the representation of your choices so far. The choices you've chosen led you here. Start making better choices if you want to get to better places.

I am currently in this growth mindset where I ask myself, "What's next?" and not tell myself. I can relax now. I've come this far. I've done enough.

I am no stranger to storms. I am no stranger to adversaries. I might fall. I might fail. I might break down and struggle to climb back up sometimes. But I will never stay down. I know my own inner strengths. I am familiar with my own endurance and resilience power. I always get back up and pull through, no matter what. That won't change today. Now, I rise again up again.

I *am tired. I am comfy. I am warm. It's cold outside. I have had a busy week,* you might find yourself thinking in your comfort zone. But does your goal matter? Does your happiness matter? Yes. Are you physically paralysed? No. Are you immobilised? No. Are you neutralised? No. Then show up for your goal or shut up about it. But before you choose to stay in that warm bed, remember your naysayers won't shut up about you quitting if you don't show up. What's it going to be now?

I learned that discipline is the most powerful decision against all distractions. I learned that discipline is having the wisdom to decline distraction, no matter how tempting, and accepting to stay focused on what must be done, no matter how I feel. I learned that discipline is not the absence of distraction but the presence of resilience. It is knowing that distraction is available and accessible but understanding that it matters less than the work I got up today to get done.

I learned that I have to elevate the level of my effort to experience the manifestation of my expectation. I learned not to be frustrated because I am not seeing anything substantial in my life yet. You see, progress is about being better in the present than you were in the past. Even if it is by a year, a month, a week, or a day, it still counts. You just have to get up again and do it all over with intent.

I could have settled for the good life. I could have settled for a safe life. I could have settled for the 9-5. But I learned that safety diverts us from our true potential and destiny. Working on what you desire is where your happiness will come from. There is no safety in settling for less. There is no safety in holding on to what you've got if you desire to evolve in life. You can't get far by hiding behind mediocrity. In short, safety traps us in sadness. In stress. Distress. In darkness.

I have learned not to be in a constant search for what I want but to pause to remind myself of who I am and who I have become. I learned that achievement is awesome but is pointless without the enjoyment of it. And we can't enjoy our achievements if we are constantly focused on the next journey in life. I learned that the fastest way to misery is trying to get somewhere every day, but the quickest way to happiness is working on being in a better place mentally, every day. We are not designed to rush through life, we are designed to process life, day by day. Those who find themselves having a mental breakdown do so because they are always in a rush to get somewhere at the expense of experiencing the present moment that they are in.

Another day, another way forward, I see. We all have busy lives. We are all tired. We all feel fed up with many things in life. But some of us never stay down. We are never found giving up. We always look forward to getting up, to shaking ourselves to the realisation that we made it through yesterday, so what more can stop us now? Nothing can stop me ever. And so far, it has been worth it all.

Today is such a beautiful opportunity to take me further, so I am thankful that I am back on track, working hard, filling up the cracks, and not panicking. Seeing even the littlest progress is a solid inspiration for success. You see, success is but the sum of little steps. These steps are like slices of a whole pie. And until we have tasted the progress of that first step, we won't see the need to want more of it. In short, it is never too late to begin or to get back on track. But, not to get back on tract when you know you can if you really want to is one way to admit defeat.

Today, I urge you to have a taste of your values too. When I inspire others, I don't forget that I, too, need to be inspired. So, I discipline myself each day not just to be an inspiration to anyone but to experience in my own life what it means to be inspired by me. I demand more from myself. I do this by investing more time into my life to practice and experience what I teach and believe in. I extend this perspective by not just being useful to others but also being helpful to myself. I pour into myself what others are happy taking from me. And I do so with this motto:

You can't give a customer what you won't eat to eat.

A motto that helps me maintain my standards high. And in whatever I do with my life, I never fail to apply my values on a personal level. I don't just watch my fruits ripe and let others tell me how juicy they look or how amazing each bite they take makes them feel. I, too, take from my tree and taste my own fruits.

In the past, I have been too hasty to act, I failed to think, and I failed to make better decisions. It cost me a lot more than I would want to repeat. Now I understand that the collaboration between thoughts and actions solves the most challenging problems. Of course, action has many advantages, but action can never be used as a substitute for thinking. We have a brain for a reason, like hands and legs. Think so that you can make better judgments and decisions in life.

I talk less and take more action. I wish less and work more towards my goal. Because I am aware that I can wish for it all I want. I can pray for it all I like. I can talk about it all I care. But I won't get to my goal until I start putting consistent effort into it. So stop talking about it. Be about it. Become it.

I like sleeping longer. I like staying up late and watching movie after movie. I like binge-watching series. I like spending all my day on social media or partying with my friends. But I love a better life for myself. And none of those approaches have worked so far. I know that I have a choice to choose between what I like and what I love. I wake up differently because I love nothing more than to achieve a better life. A lot of us want change, but we are not ready to change how we apply ourselves each day. Change requires sacrifice, and sacrifice requires doing without what you felt like you couldn't live without before.

Today, be different. Not perfect. I used to feel scared of expressing myself. I used to be worried that when people heard me speak, they might think I was a joke. But, at some point, I realised that we are all different, and being different is powerful. I realised that I might not be perfect, but being different attracts and inspires. I realised that being different is what makes each one of us stand out and makes people wonder, *what's so special about this one? I need to know more.*

Why do I show up every day? Honestly, some days I don't want to get up. Some days I don't want to show up. Some days I don't want to work hard, but when I think about that last version of me I swapped for this guy right here, I never want to go back to who I was so desperate to change.

I got up and showed up today because I recognised that there must come a point in life where growth isn't about being tough or gentle with myself, but being a grown-up and being fair to myself. For this reason, I tell myself this: **make better choices or face the consequences.** I hold myself accountable these days As much as I celebrate a great day at the office. I don't leave myself room to play the victim anymore. If I mess up, It is back to the drawing board for adjustments and improvements. If I get the day right, I celebrate and enjoy the moment.

Today I invite you to think before you ignore a better choice. If your inaction doesn't help your goal, don't make that choice, don't do it. Before I decide not to do something, I always consider the future consequences of it. Will my inaction lead to a bad outcome? I ask before I decide. You see, from my experience, I learned that the foresight of consequence keeps us in line. The thought of consequence keeps us committed and focused. Consequence makes us show up.

I stopped sacrificing my happiness to please anyone and started putting myself first so I could be a great source of my own happiness. I learned that people might free willingly stick around to enjoy life with you when things are good, but they are not obligated to stay and suffer with you when things get tough. And often, nine out of ten, they leave. The only person that can't or won't leave you is you.

IV

LIFE

Live it before you have to leave it.

SOME SPECIFIC FRIENDLY ADVICE & LIFE LESSONS LEARNED THROUGH LIVING BETTER

Life teaches a selective few a lot of things, so it doesn't have to teach everyone else everything all over again. Here's what I can pass onto you from my life . . .

I take pride in my pain because I have learned that pain isn't always a bad thing. It can also be a blessing. It might come at a bad time or make us look weaker than we are at times, but pain turns us into powerful people. I learned that when we go through pain, we are provided with an opportunity to seek out what more can become of us, and through that, discover life's pleasures and peace.

I learned that my priority of the day has to always be to feel better rather that to achieve more. I learned that it is better to have peace, pleasure, passion and purpose in life than to have more possessions. I learned that I don't have to do anything I don't want to do even if it is going to benefit me, but I also learned to be wise in my choices. To choose to do something different everyday if I don't want to wake up feeling the same: sadness, anger, exhausted, unhealthy, unloved, unappreciated, or unbothered everyday.

I learned that in order to be great, you have to let go of being good. You can't be good and great at the same time, both are at a different level, and you can't be in two places at once. So, choose what you want to let go of today and go for what you want right now.

But, I don't know what to do with my life, many might argue. *Life is so complicated*, some might add. Here is the thing; life is pretty straightforward in what it wants you to do with it. All it wants you to do is:

Love yourself in it.

Improve your past in your present through it.

Vow to make amazing memories with the people you love in it.

Enjoy every moment of it till your very last breath.

I have learned to know the difference between moving on from something and moving through it. I have learned not to assume that everything is my job to fix or change. I have learned that some things are not changeable just because they were once valuable to us. I have learned that sometimes my inability to break through a situation is because there isn't any profitable way behind the obstacle in front of it.

I learned that some paths aren't made to lead anywhere else that is for us. I learned that sometimes what we need, we won't find where we thought we might get it from. I learned that rejection can be a good sign to change direction after a duration of effort. I learned not to waste too much time asking questions where answers aren't forthcoming: **some things we just can't change no matter how much we challenge them.** So, there's a point in life where letting go and moving on are the smarter choices to make. You just have to learn to know it.

I learned that my progression never needed anyone's approval. Just my permission to see me as my own possession and project. Yes, I own me, and I owe me. And as soon as I started giving myself more time, I started seeing myself become more than ever before. I started feeling heard. I started completing the goals I once dreamt of. I started becoming what I thought I would never be: happier!

I learned that some people have a nice figure but they haven't figured themselves out or their life out. And when they eventually age they become sad, and depressed because the human body is doomed to perish. And through this revelation I learned that ageing is inevitable, so as I age, I learned to cherish the vitality of my mentality over my body's physicality. I learned that I can't stop my body from ageing but I can prevent my mind from diminishing as I grow older. I learned that my mind is my best leverage for all versions of my future self. I learned that as we age our body stops being a source of happiness. As we age, we ache and as we ache we become less mobile. I learned that as we age, we become less willing, less eager, less wanting to exercise, more aware of our insecurities. I therefore learned to exercise not primarily for the superficial look but for the internal longevity of my mindset's vitality. I learned that being physically muscular won't take my insecurities away. I learned that looking muscular might conceal my insecurities but it can never cancel them.

Before I start each day, I always remind myself to taste every minute of my day like a drop. I remind myself to hold my cup with both hands and not spill what's in it. I remind myself not to waste any drop of it because there is no refill after life ends. So today, I say to you also, ***TASTE EVERY MINUTE OF YOUR DAY LIKE A THIRST-QUENCHING DROP!*** Don't rush around with a cup of what's left of all you've got. Take a deep breath, don't let the past distract you from what's ahead. Don't hesitate, and don't be in haste. Don't waste your day carelessly, don't spill your day aimlessly. Just take a step at a time and keep steady. Life is your cup, and what's left in it is all you will get. Taste each day like a drop.

Pull the plug out of your feelings, get off the sofa and make today about you. Do whatever you want but do something that is worth it. Something that counts. Make it about your health. Make it about your happiness. Make it about those kinds of moments that bring you pleasure. Whatever it is, just make it happen today.

The mess you are in conceals valuable lessons you need to become the best version you can be. Don't just feel the pain. Let it fill you with wisdom. You learn the most when the bright colours peel off your face, when your back is against the wall, when the glass that holds your water shatters, leaving you thirsty. When your health fails your body, when pain is all you can feel and hurt takes the place of where happiness once resided: your heart. When you are in a mess, you learn how pain can help you navigate away from future self-sabotaging.

I learned that every yesterday becomes a past today. I learned that we are strengthened through what we've been through. And being here today means that you've survived your past. So, don't let your pain own you. Don't let your past own you. Own them. You might not have created them, but being here today means, one way or another, you conquered them. Own that victory. It is all your doing!

Some days I choose to be gentle with myself. Some days I am not so subtle with myself. This is because I learned that sometimes becoming requires force. And sometimes, just a natural flow of things to be is all I need to let happen. The most important thought is this: I am always stepping forward, and when I become the obstacle in my way, I let instinct lead me into what to be: **gentle** or not so **subtle**.

I learned that doing more than before is a success: picking myself up when I lost motivation. Picking myself up when I fell—talking myself out of quitting. I fought that part of me that considered me weak and lazy. As a result, I am doing pretty much better than I thought. Before, I would have quit at the first sign of discomfort. All these I also call success.

I learned that hardship makes us invisible. I learned that hardship makes us undesirable. I learned that it is not unusual for people to stop noticing you during your toughest times in life. To stop being around you. It is not okay for that to happen to you, but it will be okay even if no one supports you. It will be okay even if no one recognise your battles and daily effort. It will be okay even if no one asks you how you are, while you are going through the toughest battles in your life. I know you will get through it okay. Just don't give up on yourself, okay? I hope your answer is yes, I won't give up on me. You might be all you've got, but I promise you, you are enough to get you through your suffering.

Over the years, I have fallen into this beautiful habit of saying kind words to myself daily. And, through it, I shine daily. I learned that happiness is self-devotion and conviction. It is looking into the mirror and telling the person that you see something daily like this: *you have been through a lot lately. You deserve happiness. You've earned it, with hurts, with rejections, with failures. I will help you get it.*

Stick to your intentions and plans today whether you feel like it or not. Be in control of your impulse and silence the noise of your impulse when it speaks into your body and mind. Impulse derails growth. Impulse destroys opportunities, and impulse disrupts happiness. Don't let impulse win today. Go Champ.

Have the urgency to proceed but don't be in a hurry to make it. Don't be in haste to have it. Haste creates mistakes. Mistakes create hesitation to take another big step. Hesitation creates fear. Fear creates doubts. Doubt creates discouragement. Discouragement creates inconsistency, and inconsistency creates discrepancy, which eventually leads to quitting.

Today be present with intent. Suit up for the life you are built for. Don't let that unique candle you are burn down daily for nothing. Your flame won't burn forever. Show up to own the spotlight. Light the room with your essence. You are one of a kind. In you is a fire of greatness. So please, don't be lazy with it. Let it blaze. Let the world feel its presence.

At some point, the quality of your work will play a role in your success. But right now, it is the quality of your character that will bring you to your success. So focus on being more patient, focus on being more proactive. Focus on being more protective of your peace. Focus on being more productive and creative. Focus on being more knowledgeable. Focus on being more helpful and valuable. These are the characteristics that sharpen our probability of breakthroughs.

Every day is a new place to venture into and experience something new. Don't stay in a place just because it is familiar and you are scared of the unknown. Yes, familiarity holds security, but the unknown keeps better promises. By all means, enjoy where you are, but find joy in where else you can be. It is okay to try new things and to feel out of place. However, clinging to familiarity can cost you opportunities. And yes, you might feel lost and out of place, but when you feel out of place, you are merely in a new place of experience—venture forth. Don't panic. There is always something of magic and meaning when we look at where we've never looked before.

I have learned that sometimes the past breaks us down so we can start a new page rather than mend it like a broken shoe. I learned that sometimes starting all over is what I was meant to do, not hold on to the hope of finding the missing puzzle to what's fallen apart in my life. Some things are not designed to be fixed but end once they've served their purpose in our life. To hold onto the hope that they might help us any longer is to hold ourselves back from what will make us happier in life.

I wake up early for my peace. I wake up early for my plan. I wake up early for my passion. Many people start their day in a rush or sluggishly because they either have no time when they wake up, or they have no purpose to get up for. But you, be different. Wake up early to have more time and wake up with a plan filled purposely. A lack of either will leave you the same or worse at the end of this year.

Why does it matter that we get better and not stay the same or worse? It matters because otherwise, we miss so much of our potential. We miss so much of a life free of pain and life's best pleasures. We miss so much of a heart full of hopes and dreams. We miss so much of what can heal us by allowing what hurts us to keep happening to us. Get better so you don't miss this much in life.

From experience, I learned that our action controls the direction of our reality, and our thoughts control our actions. But we can control our thinking. Therefore we can control our actions. Therefore we can control the outcome of our reality. For this reason, I share an observation that the first thing you have to control when you wake up is your thought, not your body. Thoughts are so powerful. They affect every area of our lives, from our body and mind to our feelings. Thoughts decide what happens next from the moment we open our eyes. To take control of any area of your life, you must first take control of when and how you wake up. You must do things that most people don't. Like waking up before everyone else and not dragging your feet throughout the day as if you are life's victim.

If only you understood your power to change yourself, you wouldn't suffer the way you have been all this while. The good news is that it is not late to understand. Neither is it too late to discover how to stop your suffering. But how fed up are you with what's hurting you? You see, healing requires you to want it bad enough. So you must stop feeling sorry for yourself and stand up for what you desire.

When you don't take time out for a break, in no time, you will break down and burn out. The signs that tell us when enough is enough can come as sudden demotivation, a lack of inspiration, and unproductivity, being unresponsive to personal obligations, frustrated with oneself, feeling deep sadness, anxiety, emotional instability and sleeplessness (insomnia).

Over the years, I have learned never to let yesterday's disappointment discourage me today in pursuing personal growth. I learned not to escape the possibility of another failure by facing my challenges once again, despite past experience. Instead, I learned to use those experiences as indicators that I am almost there and not where I started. And by doing so, after a while, suddenly, I began to find myself exceeding my past results.

The moment I realised that I was capable of positively changing my life, that I was no exception to what's possible and what's doable, it was a no-brainer. I had to get started. And starting brought me to this magical state of self-awareness and happiness today.

Make it a mission never to give up on your goal. You see, the real success in any achievement is not the physical result but the awareness that you endured the challenging process it presented you with The mental development in toughness and resilience. Because that mental realisation will become the key to achieving your next big goal.

We often miss our opportunity for greatness because we don't make self-belief a personal responsibility. But, when you strongly believe in yourself, every other opinion about your dream becomes ineffective and dismissed.

I brought my idea into existence by visualising what I wanted as if it was already tangible among those of my competitors, and then I valued the idea to the point that it became one of the most essential things on my mind every day until it happened. So, to you with a big goal or dream, see your goal as if it has already happened. Visualise it as if it is with you, or imagine what it would feel like when it does, and hold onto that beautiful feeling every waking hour of your day.

You see, what we think of the most and work on the most eventually manifest.

I keep on going and winning in life because I have learned never to stop betting on myself even when I am scared. I have learned to never stop betting on myself even when I am down. I have learned to never stop betting on myself even when I am left with crumbs and can't afford to cover the essentials. I have learned to never stop betting on myself even when the shoes become too tight to walk in and my brain wants to quit. I have learned to never stop betting on myself even when my body turns against me. I have learned to never stop betting on myself even when I have no handle on my happiness. I have learned to never stop betting on myself even when no one thinks I am good enough. I have learned to never stop betting on myself even when I can't find the push in me some days. I have learned to never stop betting on myself even when I am alone. I have learned to never stop betting on myself even when my grass doesn't look colourful, even when my job or my life doesn't give me satisfaction. So, in whatever hardship you find yourself at this point in your life, that ship will inevitably sail if you never give up on yourself.

Listen up, don't let the tune of life play out on you. Listen to the sound of your own dream and dance to it till you will your prize. Stop spacing out on the couch, wishing for a lucky day, day in and day out. This is your only life. There is no backup. There is no second life. Whether you live your life scared or you live it taking risks that align with your desires, it won't change the ending: death. Each day you get to see is the only one that you can make a difference in. Don't let hesitation eat your years away. Get up and live your heart out before the tune of life plays out on you.

I learned to enjoy now as if it's the last one of my gracious life. I learned accept that now is all I am allowed to say with confidence, that, yes, *this is my life, I am alive*. Tomorrow will always come, but today might be my last day before it. So, like me, make it count as if it is your final day left, because it could eventually be the last day of your whole life.

In between working hard, I press my timer and time myself for randomness. I take off my seriousness hat and take a break to get distracted. I scroll, like, love, laugh, and laze around for a bit. Then I get back at my goal. Getting to any destination is all about balance. You can't keep going going going. Otherwise, everything else fun in your life will be gone. At some point, you must stop to breathe. To check on everyone and everything else so you don't lose track of other vital things that make life worth fighting for.

Escaping is a wall that keeps us far away from happiness. You see, it is okay to have a break when you feel crushed, but remember to go back and face what broke you down. For you can't fix what you fail to face in your life. Many of us find it easier to keep escaping a life that weighs on us, but running away from our problems keeps us trapped through them. To break away, we can't keep running away from what we must face and fix.

I learned that those who wanted me to be perfect didn't deserve the best of me. I learned that perfect is another word for pressure and stress. I learned that perfect is another word for limitation. I learned that perfect is another word for being controlled, delayed, or diverted from enjoying every moment of my life. I learned that perfect is another word for being drained, overworked, used, and abused. I learned that I am only trying to be perfect to be accepted by others that find use in me, not for me to be happy. I learned that I never once required myself to be perfect for me. And once I started being me for me instead of being perfect for others, I started feeling more joy, more peace, more love, more self-value, and more self-confidence. So, be you, not perfect.

When life got tough for me and my back was against a spiky wall, I could have backed down. I could have had a meltdown. I could have broken down and stayed down. I could have given up. But because I knew my life was my own choice to make, I decided not to break down. I decided I was going to break through that wall instead. And that is how I found myself on the other side of what was once my wall.

My turning point in life was realising that I was worth more than my job, worth more than my past, and worth more than others' opinions of me. I was worth more than the version of me who thought I wasn't worth more than a life of existence and not one of exceptionality.

Today, it is only equity. It is not a permanent possession. But what you make with it is yours to keep. So, don't be inactive with it, don't stay the same, and idle in it. Make something out of today that you can keep for yourself. Don't cram everything you want to do or feel into this one day. Don't stop, but take it slow. Don't do too much that does not involve you. Don't rush your heart pointlessly. The day will end either way when the time hits 12am. So, feel every tick on the clock, feel every second of it that goes by. Let every minute of it serve as a stepping stone into the next adventure of your life.

Truth is, to have what you see now, I had to become my own destination. I became my own attraction. I became my own addiction. I became my own selection. I had to make myself matter so I could make myself better. So, if you want this also, you must become obsessed with your progress in this season that you are in. And the work must start now. You must get up for it. Dress up for it. And keep showing up.

You are a great seed, and this moment that embraces your being is the greatest soil of growth. So let yourself feel the space of this moment, fall into it with every inch of yourself and do well to rise up when you leave it.

To those who aim to have a peaceful and productive day, take note of this. Activity does not always equate to profitability. So, be mindful of what you do today. Don't just do anything without a sense of the order of importance, but first, do the important things that take away pressure from your life and add value and peace to your life. Priority, you see, is important to progress. So don't start the day without a to-do list of priorities to do.

Starting my day with a plan gives me a sense of control over the important things in my life. And also an opportunity to deal with unexpected matters without the extra weight of stress and pressure. Plans might not always work out, but you've got nothing to lose by making a plan and way too much to lose by stepping into a world full of unexpected and unforeseen surprises.

Stop moaning about how unfair life is. Throw away that sense of emotional dependency and own your responsibility to be happy and follow your heart's request with your best. And when you do start, enjoy every bit of the process. Be proud and patient. Allow yourself the time to grow. Don't moan. Stop asking how long. Do it for as long as it needs to be.

Stop beating yourself up and calling yourself a loser or a failure. At some point in life, everyone hits rock bottom. How we push ourselves back up starts with letting go of feeling unfairly treated by life. Push that sense of victimhood away. You have qualifications, and so what? Qualifications can't stop you from hitting rock bottom in life. There is a clear difference between having good grades and good guidance in life. The latter is what will help you advance back up. Who told you that education could prepare you for life? No one could ever figure everything about life out in a classroom full of books and intellect. We might have millions and billions of books teaching about life on this planet. But life is bigger than one planet. So, you see, education will teach you facts, but only life can teach you feelings and their mysteries. So, learn from your own experience and that of those who have mastered the bottom and the top in life. That way, you are guaranteed to advance from rock bottom when you eventually find yourself there.

I learned that in life, we can't fix everything. Sometimes we are stressed because no matter how much we've tried something that we once had worked for us. But take note, sometimes what's broken doesn't always need fixing, but replacing with something new. Yes, by all means, fix what you can, but understand that some things are in your life not to be fixed but to fix you, and when its time is done, you must let go and move on.

LIFESTYLE

Let every part of you that keeps you in existence experience the best that you can become.

I have learned not to hate my life when times are hard. I have learned to accept that life can't always be good. I have learned that good times are born from tough times. In fact, I love hard times. These days I seek them out. I embrace them because hard times once taught me how to appreciate the good times when they come around.

To those who are being rushed and crushed under the weight of a to-do list, and have no time to take a breath, do well to remember this: Our demise does not shrink but extends from the moment we are awake if the sole reason for waking up early is to have more time to do more. It must follow that the simple solution to having not enough time to live the peaceful, stress-free, joyful life you want to live is not starting early, but not starting deliberately early to think positively before you start doing anything at all.

Don't just exist. Live. Live to improve. Live to inspire. Live to interact. Live to experience. Live for the excitement. Live for your self-expression. Live to leave your mark in people's hearts when you are done. That's what it means to be alive.

Don't be in a rush to get through the day. That's how you miss out on the beauty life has to offer. Life isn't meant to be fast-paced. Life isn't meant to be joyless. Life isn't meant to be a burden to your body, heart or soul. So, slow yourself down today. Let your lungs enjoy the fresh air. Let your eyes absolve the colour of this beautiful nature. Let your ears enjoy the voices of nature's cutest and finest animals. Let your tongue soak in the taste of that earthy coffee. Let your feet feel the comfort of your own shoes. Let the little beautiful things keep hold of your senses for a little longer.

Be excited about today. Be excited about converting every minute of it into your advancement. Be excited about the new experiences you can have. Be excited about the new possibilities you can create. Be excited about the new limits you can break. Be excited because today is here to help you get to where you deserve to be in life.

Happiness is not about getting more but being grateful for what you have. So, today, I urge you to count your blessing. I urge you to look at what you have and not what you don't. You see, often we are sad because we let others dimmed light distract us from our glow. We miss our bliss in life because we are too busy looking at the missing pieces and not the presence of the many blessing within.

Don't ignore your **BODY**, **MIND** or **SOUL**. Your body, your mind and your soul all coexist to keep you alive. You can't ignore any one of them and expect a better life. You must spend an equal amount of time on them all. You don't have to do it all at once. But the time you spend on each one of them must be fair and balanced.

If you want to win against stress today, go easy on yourself. Take a calm breath with each step. Don't go faster than you can go, and neither should you go slower than you can go. Just keep moving in a way that allows your body, mind and soul to keep up. A pace that isn't crazy or lazy but mindful, gentle, collective, and calm.

I treat every day as if it is coming to an end, even before it begins. This gives me a sense of urgency that I don't have much time left to get things done. So now I have no choice but to mentally or physically categorise all I need to do and then prioritise what's important and then filter off distraction, so I can maximise my output for that day.

This morning, God gave me grace, but my growth, that's definitely all on me. So, I won't put what I am or where I am, or how I look today on the high calories in the junk foods I ate. I won't put how I feel on my past pain. I won't put what I didn't get done on the 12 numbers on my clock. I won't put how much I can earn on my boss. I won't put how much I can learn on my coach or teachers. I put it all on me.

Flawlessness is not a prerequisite for happiness. Same as getting your life together does not require you to be perfect first. To be happy, you can have flaws and still be good enough. You just have to start with how you are today and keep working on improving every version of you that you wake up to daily.

You are not obliged to burnout. You are not obliged to be overwhelmed and overworked. You don't have to crash in the name of money. You don't have to lose your health in the name of achievements. You are no good sick. You are no good stressed. You are no good sad. Be wise enough to know when to:

Slow down.

Take a few deep breaths.

Off your mind.

Pour peace and pleasure into you.

HARD TRUTH

Healing comes from the heard truth.
So, keeping it real is what can heal us.
Everything else only pokes and peels at our pain.

You are not defined by the years you've lost

You are not defined by the things you never had.

You are not defined by the environment that let you down. You are not defined by the community that gave you less. You are not defined by the life you never had. You are not defined by the past that wasn't great. You are not defined by the childhood that gave you such torturing traumas. You are not defined by the rejection you've had. You are defined by what you want to be defined by. You are defined by the direction of your desire. So, choose a desire to be defined by, that's where your happiness lies. Direct yourself towards it. Chase it and conquer it.

I learned that facing and enduring the worst in life empowers us to get the best from life. It will be uncomfortable. It will be dreadful. It will be hurtful. It will overwhelm you, but it will never overpower you if you don't allow it to. Pain is inevitable. But it serves a purpose in our life if we dare to learn from it and grow through it. It might be hard to accept that the pain from our suffering offers us a new level of strength. That the pain of discomfort offers us a new direction. That the pain of heartbreak offers us a new path in life. That the pain of struggle offers us better endless possibilities. But, it does. Pain is a necessity, it prepares us for progress, offers clarity to our current calamity, and prepares us for the future. This is simply why we go through a lot. Do not let your pain get the best of you. Become your strongest self through it.

Life goes on. And life ends. Yes, it is never too late to start living your best life, but those words don't make you immortal. Death is an unchangeable event. So, begin to live your life now while you are still alive and full of life. Let go of the things you can't change, and enjoy the freedom of your capacity to change the things that will make the rest of your life enjoyable.

You are the author of your own life. And, each day you live in is a story plot. Suppose a lot of what goes into it isn't what you want. Suppose you are struggling because you haven't been fighting to end it, you might want to change your **struggle** or your **title**. But, if you still want to keep your job, be in charge, change what isn't working, and be the boss of your life.

You become your obstacle to happiness when you stay too long where you don't belong. But good things come to those who wait. Some might argue, perhaps you too. But the truth is, enduring what you are fed up with in the hopes things might change for the better isn't being **patient**. It is being **complacent**. And, complacency is the foundation that holds the wall firm that keeps us trapped from a life of freedom and happiness.

One of the unspeakable truths is that until you do something about it, you still want everything in your life that you don't want. You see, action speaks louder than complaining. Our circumstances do not bind us. We are bound to our reality by the actions we don't take.

You can run, but you can't hide, you can escape, you can ignore, and you can procrastinate, but you will never be set free from the problems in your life until you face them and resolve them.

The heaviest weight you will ever lift up is your mind. Lifting my mind up when my body wants to stay down has strengthened my body.

To be the hero of your happiness, you must be the villain of your pain, not the victim. When you rise above and beyond your pain, you defeat it once and for all.

At some point in your life, if you wish to be happy, you have to face your fears, your doubts, your uncertainty, your inner critics, and your outer critics, and silence them for good. So start the day by facing your issues. Don't avoid them in an attempt to escape them. Involve yourself in them so you can resolve them for good. Escaping is not a remedy. Escaping is not ending. Escaping is not healing. Escaping is not resolving. Escaping is prolonging. Escaping is worsening. Escaping is sabotaging.

Neglect is not a solution nor is it a defense against our agonies. I learned that it isn't bright to leave out doing what I should, because neglect brings no delight. I learned that neglect is fertile; it is the mother of misery and tragedy. Its impact might not be visible instantly but, slowly and surely, its effect is inevitable. I learned that neglect is a process where we permit ourselves to give birth to sadness and suffering: A tragical way to voluntarily fall apart. And when we neglect to do what we can do, what we should do, or what we must do, just because we don't feel like it today, we surrender our strength and invite suffering and sadness into every room of our home (body, soul, heart, and mind). I learned that suffering and sadness only stop when we are as good as we need to be at any time, every day, not when we only get up and show up to do better when we feel good. So to you who want to live a much better life today than you did yesterday, never neglect what you must correct. Respect yourself enough to erect your falling building. You see, neglect is not primarily the art of doing nothing, neglect is a performance of avoidance and life is an observant audience. You get the reaction of how well or badly you've done on the stage where life is watching you. Life is always watching you. Do what you can do. Do what you should do. Do better.

The fear of the truth is a way to self-sabotage yourself. Often it is not what we want to hear that we need to hear. Our ears are strong enough to take anything. Our heart is strong enough to keep beating regardless of any harsh truth. So, we can take it, and since we can take it, what's there to fear, but the pointless threats of fear itself!

I learned that life is not a take-it or leave-it kinda thing. Life is a make it as you see fit, it is a mean it and you will manifest it. It is a here is the pen and paper (will power). Write your story if you fancy. The how is up to you. The when it up to you. The who is up to you. The where is also up to you. It is up to you to be silly or sensible with what story you write. And before I forget, life does want you to succeed as much as it brings about things that might break you down. So, you see, shit does happen, sometimes. Sorry, a lot of times! So, learn to be in a constant state of empowering your mindset with lessons and wisdom through not being scared to live life, and taking risks, to gain valuable experiences, so you become equipped to fix things up when you do screw up. You will screw up at some point. It is inevitable. But, you can survive it and thrive because of it, if you don't stop learning and growing through anything life throws at you.

Don't be comfortable with what is not making you happy. You either end it or have no choice but to keep enduring it. But to endure what you prefer to end is to accept that your peace and happiness are less worthy of your effort to make the change.

One of the reasons we can't find the solution to our problems or happiness is that we don't look for ways to add value to who we are. You simply have to be involved in your life to evolve it. So if you are not part of the equation, you are part of the problem. Your answers start with challenging you to change you.

We remain stuck and sad in life because we avoid digging up what we know we need to know to avoid facing the truth of the matter weighing on our minds. But, to get what you want out of your life, you have to be honest with yourself. You have to take a step back and be objective about what's not working in your life, that's how you can find out the why. You might not like the answer. You might not know what to do about it when you find out. But that is the key to fixing things. The why always directs us towards the path of result that will change it all.

If you consider yourself too busy and don't have time to build yourself, this is the truth: *you don't have too much to do, you just think too little of yourself.* There's always going to be someone in a worse position than you but doing better than you, someone less strong but working harder than you, and someone with less opportunity but creating more chances than you. Your excuses are only as strong as you make them out to be.

Any moment in every moment you show up could be your moment. So, show off with 100% energy commitment and dedication when you show up. For many years I was counted out, told I wasn't good enough, told I didn't have any purpose, and told to do what I was told. I was told that I belonged to those who settled for less. I kept on showing up, nevertheless. I showed up hopeful, humbled, and grateful. I never fumbled the chance to put my best on display at any task, and each time I did my best, I exceeded expectations. My energy was unquenchable and unquestionable. That I made sure no one could argue against or compete against. Then one day, it all changed with one yes. With one, I love his energy. I love his commitment. He deserved to be chosen to represent us and himself. Any day could be the day someone important is watching you. So every day, show up at your best no matter how small or big the task is. All it takes is one yes. All it takes is one moment of your best at its full display.

I know better today than I did yesterday. So, I accept that change will always happen, regardless of whether I want it. But I will take the steps others fail to take during this new season of change. Turns don't wait forever. Seasons don't stay forever. I am mature enough to know that no heart beats forever, so yes, a new season might come again, but what's the guarantee that when it does, I might finally be in a position to take advantage of it? None. So now, I promise I will continue improving with change. I won't stay the same ever again. I hope you do the same too today.

If they can make it happen, I can do it too. If I can make it happen, you can make it happen too. This was how it all started for me. In retrospect, all we need to succeed in life is never to count ourselves out of what's possible, even where it feels impossible. You see, impossibility is merely a fairy tale told by the likes of fear and doubt. Great men and women of all eras have shown us that everything is possible with belief. It is always a remarkable story not just to prove that everything we think and imagine can manifest but to reaffirm that possibility is not a thing of myth but of faith. But also to empower us to realise that none of us is an exception to bringing what's in our imagination, no matter how bizarre it might seem, into the reality we all live in.

When you are hard-working, people will call you lucky. But only you know what hell you went through to get here well. So let no one get to your head or your heart. Stay humbled. Stay cool-headed. Stay laser focused. Keep on going. Keep doing your thing: *winning, healing, succeeding.*

If you are not doing what you should be doing, then you are doing what you shouldn't do. And doing what you shouldn't be doing will take you off track from where you should be going. So do what is right, do what you should. Stay on track, stay disciplined. That is how you get to arrive where you want to be.

Complaining is that voice that tells us through us that we are not in charge, and it does nothing more than suggest that we have no power over the circumstances that we are presently facing. Action on the other hand implies that we are not going to let our circumstances dictate our future and destiny. In order words we are not just sitting in the driver's seat, but we are in control of where next to go.

I am at that stage in life where I stop spending all my time looking nice and start balancing my time in a way that allows me to be more than I look. I want to feel other sensations in my lifetime not just the weight of the muscles on my body. I want to feel real wellness and happiness. I want to experience real rewards from the risks I take in life. I want to manifest real energy from the excitement of what else I can become as a person. I want to feel real pleasure not just from pain, but also from love, peace, calm, or rest. I want to feel things I can still feel no matter what age I get to. For these reasons, I don't train my body crazily; I just train to be healthy. My inner health is more long-lasting than how I look on the outside.

When we do what's challenging repeatedly, it becomes almost effortless indefinitely. Believe it or not, you are the most important person in your life right now. You are the foundation upon which everything else stands. That includes the people that are very important to you. A weak, broken, or unstable foundation can never hold the most well-designed buildings or belongings. Without you, everything else falls apart because you are the source that powers and holds everything straight in your life. So, do well to stay well. Always.

Idleness breeds disappointment, and disappointment breeds sadness. There is always something you can work on right now. Stop waiting to know exactly what you want in before you do something today. Work on what you have until you know what you want in life. It is all connected one way or another. If you don't know what you want yet, focus on being the best at who you are now.

No matter how painful the past has been. What we do with it in the present defines who we become in the future. You can use your past to determine your greatness or deny yourself of it, depending on if you describe yourself as more potent, resilient, a conqueror by your past or as a victim because of your past.

Some disappointments are actually a blessing in disguise. Sometimes you don't get what you want when you work for it. Sometimes you lose what you have, even if you've earned it. Both times can be because you were asking for less or you were holding on to less. And to get what you deserve, every less in your life has to go first.

When you take control of your life and hold yourself responsible for how you want to feel going forward, you stop being the victim of your circumstance. Expect that many people will get crossed with you but don't react. Instead, stand firm in your decision, and hold on to what it will make of you: happiness. Anyone angry at you for choosing you is only mad because they've lost the power they once had over you.

The fear of distraction can be costly, and we suffer deeply both in body and mind because of it. So I start my days now device free. I practice discipline by investing my waking up hours into feeding my mind and body with positive things before anything else. This is one good practice of happiness to take note of.

Often it is the going, going, going, that breaks us, wounds us, and burns us out. Sometimes to heal, you need to take some time off everything else and spend every minute with yourself.

The same action every day won't give you a different outcome. So if you want to change, you have to go for the alternative of indifference. You have to start changing how you wake up, get up and show up. You have to convince yourself that starting later is too far and that you deserve better now, more than ever.

Often we lose the people we love because they are the reason we are not living our true potential. If this is you, yes, it might not be the source of the problem you expected it to be. But sometimes the people we lose are due to the prayer we once made to God to take away the obstacles in our way to a better life.

Fear has always been a part of my journey to success and this time is no different. I am not scared to take another risk. I am not scared to set another goal. I have something more powerful at my disposal: I have courage despite my fear. Courage gives me the confidence to edge further where fear seeks to stop me. Have courage!

It is okay to feel lost. It is okay to feel off-path. It is okay to make mistakes. It is okay to fail. These are not obstacles, nor the end of the road. These are vital signs that you are moving forward. That you have reached an unknown path, and that you are about to discover more than you already are. Keep going.

Don't be a victim of busyness. Don't wait till tomorrow to enjoy your life. Life has a policy of no return once you get older, and neither do you get a refund for a lesser life you don't deserve. The value of each hour does not depend on how many jobs you can get done but on how much joy you get at the end of your day. So, pause being busy and enjoy the moment you are in. Take this moment as your amusement park, and experience it as if you've paid for it, and it is about to end.

No matter how high the odds are against you. Never write yourself off. It might be hard to keep going. It might be tough not to give up when it would be a lot easier to do so. But keep believing in yourself. Keep believing in your goal. Keep believing that the universe is listening and will help you. You will get your answer soon enough.

Be gentle with how you judge yourself by others' standards and strength. Life is a struggle, no matter how good anyone makes it look, or has it. So focus on yourself and stop making your progress a competition. Stop worrying about who is doing it better than you, just keep doing your best and be proud of it. Everyone's best can look, feel, and be different. It is okay if yours isn't like others. Your survival is not a competition.

V

AFFIRMATION

*Sometimes, you have to talk yourself
out of your own negative thoughts*

MIRROR TALK

Affirmation is like a shot of endorphins. Inject it into your mind with conviction today and internalise that which you believe and become it.

Look yourself in the mirror and speak these words today:

I get up early every day because my time to be a screw-up is up. My time to be fed up is up. I blamed many people for my mess up. But, this time, the victim in me time is up. Now, I understand that clearing things up is entirely up to me. I must do this to fix myself up, so I can glow up. From today, I won't give up. I Promise.

Look yourself in the mirror and speak these words today:

I encourage what I accept. I encourage what I allow. I encourage what I am silent about: inner critic. Doubt. Stress. negative people. Today, I encourage myself not to embrace or allow these things no more.

Look yourself in the mirror and speak these words today:

Even though I don't feel like it, I will get up for it and keep at it. Because I know that it is impossible to get to where I want to be if I am inconsistent in showing up for it.

Look yourself in the mirror and speak these words today:

I am a magnetic force by nature. I control my surroundings. I push away what I don't want. I pull towards me what suits me. I don't force anything, I only attract what I want.

Look yourself in the mirror and speak these words today:

I have no fear of getting anywhere I want. I am here to get there. I have been somewhere worse before, and being right here is solid proof that I belong ahead. Now, I know that I can get anywhere. Fear can't fool me ever again.

Look yourself in the mirror and speak these words today:

Today, I will stand up for myself.

I will show up for myself.

I will step up for myself.

I will climb up for myself.

I will do whatever it takes just to see myself happy.

Look yourself in the mirror and speak these words today:

The ground below me is deep, and the wall back up is rough, but still, I choose to fly out today. And if I fall, I fall. If I fail, I fail. All I know is that these wings fluttering strong in my heart aren't for nothing. And I won't stop until I find out how far and high I can fly with them.

Look yourself in the mirror and speak these words today:

This time, no excuses. I am due this growth. I am worth the effort. I am worth the sacrifice. I am worth the fight. I will give me strength. I will make time for me. I will fight for me. I will make me proud.

Look yourself in the mirror and speak these words today:

Pain is not fearful but powerful.

Failure is not fearful but powerful.

Rejection is not fearful but powerful.

I will stop complaining about them. I will stop feeling sorry for myself about how much it hurts.

I will embrace this feeling. I will let it fuel me. I will let it empower me. And I will turn these emotions to my advantage.

Look yourself in the mirror and speak these words today:

I woke up today to cross the line of my circumstance, to take ownership and control, to make it, or to break it. Because I know that when we dare to lift the bar up, demand more, and do more, our potential and opportunities have no limit.

Look yourself in the mirror and speak these words today:

Today, I woke up feeling very courageous and ambitious. I am fully ready to start my day in the best way possible. I won't duck what's coming at me. I won't skip what I must do. I am not afraid to cross the line from my comfort zone to my war zone. I am not afraid to fail. I am not afraid to fall. I love the challenge, I love to raise the bar, so I can have my hands raised as the champion. Whatever comes to the surface of my day, I am ready to face it and defeat it.

Look yourself in the mirror and speak these words today:

This is not the time to be feeling sorry for myself. This is not the time to stay stuck in a rot. This is not the time to identify as the victim in my own story. This is not the time to say maybe later. This is not the time to feel tired and helpless. This is the time to say I got me, why not me, no one else before me, I am ready. Bring it on. Watch me bring it home. This time, it's my turn to be first, to give my best, to have the best, and to be the best. This is my turn time!*

Look yourself in the mirror and speak these words today:

My destination is my duration. Anyone's progress is not my business. I don't care who is doing better than me. I don't care who has more than me. I don't care who looks better than me. All I care about is being better today than who I was yesterday. I am my focus. I am my distraction. I am my attraction. I am my best transition. I choose myself as my only competition so I can always aim to be my best edition.

Look yourself in the mirror and speak these words today:

Yesterday might have been horrible but a terrible day does not make me less incredible or capable. Doubt me if want, but I am going for it again today. I hold myself accountable to believe that any goal I want is possible and achievable.

That's why I showed up again today, just to prove it.

Look yourself in the mirror and speak these words today:

Lord, I thank you for this graceful day. I thank you for this great health. I thank you for the support in each step I take, and for the guidance in each fight I face. I thank you for the strength and the high self-esteem. I put my intentions today in your hands. Please give me direction. Please give me more than the sight to see what's in front of me. Please give me the wisdom to help me make better choices today.

Look yourself in the mirror and speak these words today:

When I say I will make it happen no matter what. Please don't doubt me. You will only regret it.

Look yourself in the mirror and speak these words today:

I show up every day because I feel this is my season of change, and I will bloom.

Look yourself in the mirror and speak these words today:

I won't be reluctant to do what's good for my body. I won't hesitate to get up for what is good for my health. I will look after myself. I will make my body look well taken care of for me.

Look yourself in the mirror and speak these words today:

I want better health to live a better life. I want to live longer for my friends and family. I am responsible to make it happen. I love watching things on my phone. But I have self-control. I am not addicted to my phone. I am not controlled by my phone. I am not weak. I will prove it by stop scrolling now. I will get off the couch and start working on my goal.

Look yourself in the mirror and speak these words today:

Today I am in the mood to move myself to a new level.

Look yourself in the mirror and speak these words today:

I am not where I want to be yet, but I am so proud of myself that I never settled for where I used to be. I will keep going. I will wave goodbye to this version of me. I will shake hands with the next version of myself that I will produce. Nothing is going to stop me.

Look yourself in the mirror and speak these words today:

I have been following the script of my past for a while, but today it ends. I am the author of my life and not an actor in it. I am not a product of my past. I am not a product of my pain. I choose to be the producer of my circumstance not the product of it. Life happens, but what happens next when it does, that's on me. So, it is on me, as to what story comes next in this chapter of my life titled Today.

Look yourself in the mirror and speak these words today:

Start your progress with a plan. Winning starts with a plan. Without a game plan, you are out of the game before you even partake.

Look yourself in the mirror and speak these words today:

I will choose my passion over my possession. I won't let what I have to distract me from who I am born to become. I will continue to work on my potential. I will continue to create new opportunities for myself. I will continue to give my best so I can become, not just good at what I can, but the greatest at what I can become.

Look yourself in the mirror and speak these words today:

Only those who believe that they are worth more in life get up and work hard on what they want in life. So, today, I have only one thing on my mind. To put my everything in it. To make it count. To bring home a better outcome.

Look yourself in the mirror and speak these words today:

You think I am a flower? Tiny, and fragile. No no no. I am the toughest tree in the forest. So, don't bother telling me that I don't deserve to win. Don't bother making me feel less than I am. I am stronger than anything that can bother me today. And you my mind are the weakest of them all.

Look yourself in the mirror and speak these words today:

My plan for today is pretty straightforward but powerful. Never backing down from more challenging days. Working harder for better days pushes me to go further, stronger, healthier, and happier.

Look yourself in the mirror and speak these words today:

This time, victory is mine. It is all on me. It is all in me. The face of war. The shield of courage.

The spears of belief. All of it. So let the battle begin. Let it rattle me to the core. Let the storm strike like sharp spikes and the rain hit like a raging axe. Let it try to chip me away and make me fall. But, with my shield, with my spears, I will defend and strike back harder, stronger, better. I might be shaken. But I won't be broken. Defeat is not my fate. This is my war. This is my way to victory. Bring it on. Watch me win. I wake up and show up for what I want because it is me that has to live without it otherwise. I have to do it for me. This is personal. This is about my survival. This is about me, allowing myself to have the life that I know I deserve.

Look yourself in the mirror and speak these words today:

Today, I pray for the strength to control my mind. I pray for the strength to endure my pain. I pray for the strength to resist when I have had more pleasure than I should. I pray for the strength to know when to let go. I pray for the strength to be me throughout my day.

Look yourself in the mirror and speak these words today:

My plan is simple this morning. Create a purpose. Hesitate not. Dominate my doubts. Eliminate my fear. Elevate me.

Look yourself in the mirror and speak these words today:

I believed in myself.

I believed in my soul.

I believed in the rhythm of my heart.

I believed in the steps of my feet.

I believed in the strength of my mind.

And because I believed in myself, I am bound to

exceed every version of myself

in strength, health, worth,

happiness and wealth.

Look yourself in the mirror and speak these words today:

I am glad that my heart pumps blood and my brain works well. I can move my arms when I want to. I can jump when I want to. I can walk when I want to. I can attest that I am in command of these motions. I am capable of any movement I want to do. I might protest that it isn't easy to get up and go. But I can't deny that I can if I want to, I can. And if there was a big fire in my room, tiredness could never convince me not to get up and run for my life. My room is always burning, for I have a why that burns my heart with passion. And my why is my fire. And it gets me up and running every day.

Look yourself in the mirror and speak these words today:

I am in acceptance of what I am. I am also in agreement that I am built for more. I am happy with who I am today because it has been an honour to witness me grow consistently to what more I can become. I am not done yet. I am moving to what's next.

Look yourself in the mirror and speak these words today:

You might see less of me these days. You might hear neither my voice nor the sparkle between my lips. But I am not done. I am not gone. I am sown into my heart's cry for help. Growing into what I owe myself: a better me.

Look yourself in the mirror and speak these words today:

I refuse to be a victim of my circumstance today. I am not the only one that has it tough in life. But I am the only one that can get me through my tough storms in life.

Look yourself in the mirror and speak these words today:

I get up early every day because my time to be a screw-up is up. My time to be fed up is up. I blamed many people for my mess up. But, this time, the victim in me time is up. Now, I understand that clearing things up is entirely up to me. I must do this to fix myself up, so I can glow up. From today, I won't give up. I Promise.

Look yourself in the mirror and speak these words today:

Every day I wake up and make every minute count because I am worth every minute of the effort I have to put in to achieve my goal.

Look yourself in the mirror and speak these words today:

I am capable. I am constant. I am inevitable.

Just when they think I am done I Overcome. Just when they think I am down and over I rise and overflow with more. I will always keep coming, I will always keep becoming.

PART 2

I

POSITIVE CONDITIONING

*You are not your condition, but your condition is based on your mental conditioning.
Your mental condition is based on your conviction or the lack of it.*

5AM POSITIVE NOTIFICATION

If we can control our thoughts, we can control our transformation. So, pause and rest when you are tired, but don't quit because you are tired. Continue until you are transformed.

Starting your day with a positivity affirmation helps you start your day with a calibrated self-concentration, self-courage, self-control, self-connection, and a great sense of self-conviction.

From my experience and expertise, having a better life starts with being a better you, and being elite on a personal level. For this reason, I propose to you that to have an exciting life, you must become an elite person, and be unwavering in its permanent practice in your day-to-day lifestyle. On a global scale, it is well documented that early rising is a ritual for all elite individuals around the world. But more than that, starting their day early with a positive mindset is the keystone habit that sets them apart from the rest of the world. This is what separates an awesome life from an awful life: **A remarkable positive mindset**. This is why I believe that daily affirmations distinguish winners from the rest. An affirmation is not just a cool concept but a conditioning tool. It conveys qualities that enable the average mindset to upgrade into an elite mindset.

So, sometimes it is the little words we tell ourselves that make the difference between having a better day or a bitter day, hence why from the very moment I wake up, my first action of the day is to think positively and affirm that belief.

It is often suggested that positive thinking can blind us from accepting the reality that we are in for what it is. But, negative thinking offers nothing but to bind us to the reality that isn't a reflection of the better life we can have. No one thinks negatively and survives the storms of life. To think positively in any situation is not to deny or ignore that your reality is what it is but rather to inspire yourself that it doesn't have to stay that way. You can't be negative and be happy. You can't have both. But you can be positive and be happy. To think positively is to see a better outcome regardless of what situation you might find yourself in. To be positive is simply to validate a negative situation as present but to feel that you are mentally in a position to eliminate the circumstance that gave birth to that negative situation.

In practice, positive thinking is acknowledging that something awful or negative has happened but choosing not to react to it but to be in charge of how it affects you during that moment in time. Thinking positively puts you in control by giving you an alternative way to look at a bad situation. Thinking positively develops and strengthens your ability to make a resilient decision to be happy when life chooses to make you sad, mad, angry, or disappointed through bad occurrences.

Negative emotions can make us see non-threatening situations as threatening through historical association. For instance, when we've failed before, a negative mindset associates any opportunity with past failure and therefore fails to try our hand at something new. And yes, negative thinking, for instance, fear can help us avoid danger, but positive thoughts help overcome them. It is also wise to be aware that avoidance isn't prevention or resolution. Avoidance in itself can be costly as it is capable of posing a greater risk than rising up to the occasion to confront the danger in front of you, in an attempt to eliminate it for good. Negative thought puts us in a state of fear and sadness, stress, worrying, and frustration. Furthermore, a constant state of thinking negatively can lead to intense levels of sadness or depression.

Positive thoughts on the other hand can put us in a state of excitement, contentment, enjoyment, joy, etc.

Other benefits of thinking positively include the following:

- Positive thinking encourages and gives us room to think of solutions during life's surprising storms.

- Positive thinking enables us to take risks in life.

- If you can see the positive in any challenging situation, you can overcome that situation.

- Positive thinking gives us the courage to figure things out: Those who are negative fixate on the fault in front of them. Those who are positive find a way around it.

- Positive thinking makes us optimists despite adversaries: The pessimist misses the point of a setback and its benefit. The optimist gains and applies the advantage derived from it. But, those who are negative are unable to come back from a setback. They are simply devoured by it.

So, from the first moment, I wake up I always ask myself this: What positive message do I have for myself today? Once I have a picture of it, I grab a sticky note and write it down somewhere visible throughout my day. And I let that message play out in my mind over and over again. All day long. Sometimes I come up with a new one, and other times, when I don't, or when I prefer the one from the day before, I simply use it as guidance for the new day I am in.

For instance, today I thought about this one: *I can do it. I will do it. I won't quit. I won't stay down. I won't count myself out. I will make it happen. It's my turn to win. I have it in me. I will have the last fight.*

From experience, and as touched on at the beginning of this book, I learned that when we devote more time to positive thoughts, our action becomes driven by purpose, not by impulse. This explains why inspirational positive quotes are so attractive and impactful. I also learned that we can become the very source of our positive thoughts by challenging ourselves to start our day thinking positively only. And then acting according.

So, your wake-up thought is your first step to how your day will end. If you want a more productive, positive, and successful day, you must make it important to let positive thinking direct your action each day and it starts with right now. For what you think, you do, and what you do, transforms you. For this reason, I wake up with one thing in mind: to start my day with positive thoughts.

BY 5am I am primed with positive thoughts; my mind has gone through its stretches and warm-ups so to speak. By that time the morning brightens, I am up ready before many around me, to contribute meaningfully to my day, and to be ready to outwork my opponents/competitors.

5 AM is for those who are serious about changing their life for the better. Those who want to take themselves to the next level this year. Those whose goal is to be ahead in their field. It takes a different level of commitment to get up earlier than the rest, to stay up later than the rest, to think differently than the rest, and to do what the rest can do but won't do. To be the best among the rest, you must be different than the rest in how you approach your goal.

Like a lot of people, if we cared to admit it, I also live for notifications. Email notifications. Social media notifications. Text messages notification. What's new? What's happening? I wake up to it and for it all. I use to update my phone every few seconds for randomness to satisfy my boredom, and I did it for hours a week. I craved the curiosity of newness, the scrolling of more screen activities, while my life stayed inactive and negative, and nothing positive or new was happening in my life. I lived a life of comparison and complaining for a while. In my mind, I was unlucky, unlike those whose life on social media looked colourful, exciting, and glamorous.

But, I got to a point where I realised that such notifications took me away from my own reality. I was constantly excited about what to see next in the social world, but not about my own life. But, deep down, like you, I wanted to be excited to wake up for my own life too. To wake up to some good news that was for me, for my life. To make that happen, I had to change what I saw and thought of when I woke up. It had to be something that pushes me to get things done, for me. It had to be personally positively impactful. This gave me an idea of a simple proposition to help me start off my day positively: Wake up early to a positive thought by 5:00 AM and practice positive thinking throughout the day.

One thing became clear to me. Some people are not negative out of intention, but out of conditioning. Some people complain out of habit. Some find the negative in everything, just because their mind is conditioned to only see the negative and ignore the positive. That is what is happening when we can't seem to see the light at the end of the tunnel we are in. Over time, we have lost our ability to be positive: to look ahead to ending our misery and hardship. And now, even if we wish to think positively, we don't know how anymore.

Isn't this why we read self-help books? To give us that boost of energy that we can't generate ourselves? To motivate us because we can't do it on our own? I believe that it is a yes.

Below are 238 little positive quote notifications to help you prime your mind and recondition yourself to think positively no matter what situation and by so doing help you start your day great, powerful, and positive.

1.   Every day you wake up, no matter how you feel, be determined to think positively. With setbacks, stress, frustrations, disappointments, and mental breakdown being a precursor for success, there is no better strategic tool for success than developing the ability to deliberately think positively whenever, and wherever.

2.   You either rise early and start your day being in control or rise late and be controlled by life and break down fast. Choice time.

3.   When life gives you grace, you don't wait for life to give you luck and opportunity too. You don't wait for life to heal you, or cater for your basic survival needs. You go out there and get those yourself. Show up today, love yourself, and be kind to others. The world will fall in love with you.

4.   Have courage and show up. Let nothing get in the way of you and your goal today. Your fears

are merely a diversion. Your excuses are certainly a distraction. You are unstoppable. Be it! Prove it to yourself today!

5. Nothing you work on is bigger than you. Nothing you have on you is more valuable than you. Nothing you feel is stronger than you. You are superior to any terror in your life. Nothing can stop you if you focus on yourself.

6. Keep going all out even when nothing is coming in. Keep showing up even when nothing seems to be coming out of it. You are closer than you think you are.

7. Setbacks are there to test our mental strength. That's why setbacks are inevitable in life. They are unavoidable, almost unbearable, and impossible to wish away either. But what we do learn from them is that the undisciplined minds quit, but with a strong mind, you are simply unbeatable by them.

8. Not every moment has to be used for creativity, some moments are important to appreciate the producer. So today, take a moment to be proud of yourself. Take a moment to say, I am amazing. Take a moment to say, I deserve this moment of admiration and happiness.

9. If you want sustainable growth, put yourself in a room of progress and give yourself 5 years to bloom. Go through the storm. Survive the

heat. Endure the rain. And watch you rise to a new level.

10. Today, I pray for more breath, more light, more delight, more fight, more strength, more faith, more health, and more worth and growth.

11. The secret to getting ahead in life is starting before you feel like it and starting before you have no choice but to.

12. You can't wish yourself out of a rot. You can't wish your way through a mess. Waiting won't make it happen. Crying about it won't make it happen. Complaining about it won't make it happen. Wishing for it won't make it happen. Begging for it won't make it happen. Only going after it will make it happen.

13. Don't settle for what is easy. Don't settle for what is less. Fight for what you are worth. It will be worth it.

14. Stop wasting your time holding onto a life that you are better than. That isn't all there is to you and you know it. Start thinking about a life you deserve and wake up to make it happen, one day at a time.

15. Don't arrest your heart from happiness. Open your heart to the possibility of healing and you will do so. Don't deny yourself wellness by giving up hope on your healing. It is the worst

way to hurt you even more. You might be hurting today, but don't be dismayed. But it doesn't make sense to heal just to hurt again, you might protest, but hurting is more about strength and lessons, it is about the test that needs to happen to bring out the best in us. Your best is about to happen through your hurt. Keep your head up and your heart hopeful.

16. The best gift you will ever get is life and the time you give yourself, and the best gift you will ever give yourself is to experience each day of it.

17. Sometimes the only obstacle in your path towards better is your mind. Clear your mind. Clear your path.

18. There is no luck where there is no work. But where there is work, you can do without luck.

19. Dedication and discipline are the prices you must pay for what you are worth and deserve.

20. Just a little reminder. Don't rush the process. Change takes time. Change takes patience. Just keep doing your part. You will get there eventually.

21. Sometimes the only way through is to push yourself to pull yourself out of a situation that is crushing your happiness. And, yes, you might not like it. You might not be comfortable with getting

up early for it. But you must learn to show up for it if you want it.

22. No one is keeping you company? It is okay. No one is applauding you? It's okay. No one sees you working hard? It is okay. No one is checking up on you? It is okay. Sometimes it takes laying low to come back with a glow.

23. Two versions of tiredness need different approaches. If you are tired, rest. If you are fed up and tired, get up and do your best. Now go, and grow!

24. Trust the process of your growth. And do your best consistently. The process always delivers.

25. Scared it might not work? And. What if it does? It will. Go for what you want and stick with it no matter what.

26. While the day's primary objective should be to be productive, one must also seek to be positive. When we are positive, productivity flows effortlessly.

27. No matter how rough life gets, pause everything that is happening to you just to tell yourself that you are tough, that you are enough, that you are worth any price you must pay to heal.

28. While you hope for the highs to come back into your life, don't let the low period of your life

determine the glow of your day. We can be going through a difficult time in life and still find a reason to smile on any day. Look closer and you shall find out that there are many other great things present in your life that if they were absent would tear you apart.

29. Look yourself in the mirror and speak these words today: There is nothing I want that hasn't been achieved by many others before. I am no different. I will make it happen too.

30. Today, I invite you to experience every second of your existence and embrace every part of your presence.

31. When we fail to take ownership of our life and take responsibility to make them better, life punishes us with hardship. So today, I take ownership.

32. Don't lose focus because no one is around to support you, cheer you on, praise you, or approve of your work. In silence, in isolation, in darkness, behind four walls, and unsupervised, these are the places where growth usually begins and end up revealing itself.

33. Champ, what are you still doing in bed by this time?

34. Success is never going to be void of failure and setbacks. So, it is okay to fall or fail. But

don't make a home there. The bottom is there to help us stand back up, not to stay down broken. Build up the courage and get back up. Get going, and get where you deserve to be.

35. If you want more time to do more of what you love, you must start by doing more of what you love with the time you have. It is always possible to create time for what we love if we love it enough.

36. Another day. Another battle. Time to show up and settle the score.

37. Stop laying there hoping for better. Be the chaser of your dreams. Let nothing chase you down. You are the hunter, not the prey.

38. It takes a lot to push yourself through a situation that almost made you quit. Be proud of yourself. You've earned this feeling of joy and excitement.

39. I am tired of reminding you to get up and show up, but do you see me giving up on you? No. Let's go.

40. Good morning. Your tomorrow depends on you. You can't just keep wishing for it and expect it to happen. I know you are worth it, but am sorry to break it to you. If you want it, get up and work for it. It has to be earned.

41. The question is not whether you have what it takes. The question is, are you willing to believe that you do have what it takes, and make it happen? Those tough decisions I made years ago, got me through to where I am now and made life better today. Make that tough decision today. Don't wait around. You won't live forever.

42. No matter what you do today, don't leave out the part where you get to be happy and proud.

43. You don't have to kill yourself. Just keep going. Pace wins over haste, remember.

44. You wanna know what it takes to break and keep breaking limits? Your commitment. Your consistent. Your sense of self-worth. Your resilience to quitting when things get tough. And your compliance with giving it your all day in and day out.

45. How important you are to yourself is evidenced by how much time you allocate to yourself each day.

46. Before you proceed further in your process. Revise your current plan, and Adjust it according to match your current world. Great achievers are great observers and great absorbers. But most importantly they are great strategists.

47.   Be grateful today. Be thankful that you are alive. It is the most important outcome at the end of any day.

48.   Stop letting fear handicap you from the life you want to live. In front of what you are scared of is your happiness.

49.   Over time I learned that obstacles are in front of us to help us discover that we are made for more than safety and survival if we step over them with courage.

50.   Be proud of your progress continuously. Show it off respectfully so it might inspire at least one person who hasn't had anyone believe in them from day one. Let the inspired know that all it takes for them is to go for their goal. That's where genuine resilient empowerment not to give up comes from. Let the inspired know that all they need today is these four words: JUST GO FOR IT!

51.   If you want to build the life that you want. You have to be committed to your goal. You have to be committed to creating yourself. You have to be committed to showing up without fail and fail at quitting.

52.   Progress is not easy. It is not for the lazy. It is not for the uncommitted. It is not for the wisher and not the doers. Progress is for those who choose to push themselves up to show up. Those

who say, it has to happen, and it starts today, end of.

53.   Be proud of your progress so far. Show off your glow like the fruits of a tree. None of it was handed to you. You worked really hard for it. You deserve every taste of your ripeness. And so does those who inspire you to be where you are now.

54.   When you work on yourself, you become the source of your glow, and even in your darkest days, you will still be outstanding in your energy. Your vibe will stay strong. And through your presence, many will admire you and be empowered by your resilience.

55.   No matter how long what you want will take don't quit. Keep going. You are worth the healing. You are worth the work. You are worth the wait. You are worth the opportunity.

56.   Whether you show up for yourself or you don't it's up to you. But remember this: each time you do a no-show on your goal you are sacrificing your happiness, your progress, and your health. You are creating a life that you don't want, rejecting the possibility of what you desire, and accepting whatever outcome life throws at you. It is your choice today to do better just as much as it is your doing if life gets worse for you tomorrow.

57.   It takes something special in someone special to succeed. And do you know what makes

you special? Showing up despite being tired. Showing up despite failing and losing. Showing up despite nothing to show for it. Showing up without fail. Showing up because you are certain that your turn isn't far ahead. That is what makes you rare and nearer to your success.

58. Often people might think you are crazy because you are persistent with your goal. They might call you stupid for chasing a goal for years without any visible result. But often it takes an insane mind, a resistant mind, someone who would give up their stability, and their safety net in the hope of achieving something greater than themselves.

59. Are you willing to give to grow? If you are not happy right now it means that what you have isn't enough to make you happy, so why are you scared to give it up to gain something better? Why are you scared to give up your comfort zone if you are not content with your life while in it? If you really want more, you must give all that you have.

60. We all know how to quit but those who don't, don't know when to quit because they have a why that gets them up each day to do what it takes to get them where they want to be.

61. What you see is not all it is. What you see is not what you get. You get what you put into it. You get what you give up for it.

62. Today, tell yourself who you want to become with conviction: We do have a voice not just to speak to others, but to spark a fire within ourselves to evolve. Use that voice you have to push yourself up. Be the primary advocate for your achievement in life.

63. It is never a question of whether you can. It is a question of how badly you want it. That is where you will find the answer to what you want. So how badly do you want this goal in your heart? Your answer is the determinant of your success.

64. If you won't be committed to finishing it, don't wish for it. Expectations without effort will only lead you to emotional frustration.

65. To fix what's not working out in your life, you must first determine why it has to work out. Your why is the key to staying committed to your goal.

66. Push yourself today. Stop making excuses and Put your effort where your expectation is. No pressure, no pleasure. Show up. Force yourself if you have to. But do it at all costs for your sake.

67. If you can find it in you to work on your perspective so you can improve it, there is no area of your life that you can't navigate to better.

68. In your best interest, wake up and capitalise on yourself. Invest in you. You are always going to be your greatest dividend.

69. When it comes to your life, don't leave a full stop when you get stuck. Put a question. Figure it out! Stop saying to yourself. I give up. Nothing works for me. Instead, ask yourself, why isn't it working for me, and how can I give more?

70. Don't waste today being sad. It is a waste of your precious heartbeat.

71. Progress does not require you to do more than you can. It just expects you to do all that you can. Give your best today. The rest will take care of itself.

72. You are a box full of great discoveries and unlimited editions. So, don't let this version of you be all you allow yourself to be.

73. Today, my sole plan is to take care of myself. To declutter my state of mind. To stop giving people power over my smile. To protect my peace. To pursue my purpose and promote my happiness.

74. The great thing about today is that no one gave it to you, so you owe it to no one else but

yourself. So, therefore, it is yours to do as you please if you acknowledge it.

75.   Now, be careful of who enters your life. This new healing era of yours you must protect and restrict access to. The new password to your heart is peace. Only share it with those who gift you happiness like flowers when they meet you.

76.   Today, I choose me. I am not perfect. I have flaws. I make mistakes. And, I break down sometimes. But I am perfectly okay with that. I choose me.

77.   Becoming the best of yourself is not a one-day job but an everyday act. Each day you wake up and work on yourself, you create a greater version of who you were yesterday.

78.   When you don't begin you end up where you don't want to be. When you start, however, you leave the end of where you don't want to endure.

79.   One of the most rewarding feelings in life is seeing yourself grow and glow.

80.   You are nothing but unique. You are one of you, designed to be different from birth and the same till death. So, it's okay that you don't fit into the "one of us." But, you are the only original one of you.

81. If you want something different, you have to wake up differently: early, fired up, pumped up, and ready to win.

82. Stop doubting yourself. When you stop doubting yourself you start doing yourself a great favour in life. Life begins to open itself up for you in ways that were never visible or possible before.

83. Make your goal an emergency today. Make it a highly critical condition. Where there is no emergency there is no urgency. Where there is no urgency, there is no sense of immediate action.

84. You are the one person standing between what you want and what you get. If you want it bad enough you have to get out of your way and go out of your way to make it happen.

85. Stop wasting today complaining. Use that energy to show up and let your action do the talking.

86. Today, don't be emotionally lazy about the things you are physically unhappy about.

87. Be your only competition. Do your best. Rest well. And then see what's next. That's what will keep you happy. That's what gets successful people out of the bed all fired up in the morning.

88. Is what you are doing compatible with what you desire? Action does not equate achievement. Activity does not equate to productivity. Have a

game plan that is compatible with what you want and stick to it.

89.   I need a new life. No, you don't need a new life. You need a new routine. You need a new habit. You need a new perspective. You need to wake up differently, get up differently, show up differently, and do something different than your present self has done so far.

90.   At first, it was hard, but now hard hardly matters anymore. Progress has a way of making it all worth it.

91.   Today a lot of people are expecting you to quit. Disappoint them. Shut them up.

92.   The ordinary person does not get up before the extraordinary person.

93.   How you feel on any day is very important and informative, to say the least. But if how you feel will hold you back from doing something that will make you better, then how you feel becomes irrelevant in that instance.

94.   In the beginning of it, fitness is painful, exhausting, and frustrating, but at the end of the day, it is highly satisfying and rewarding.

95.   Recently I learned that personal growth could only occur when we disappear for a while, from afar, away from everything that usually takes our time away.

96. The most rewarding project you can ever work on is you. So do everything in your power to push yourself forward every single day. The process might be scary to start, it might be painful, and it might even take some while, but it will be worthwhile.

97. It becomes easy to ignore your personal needs if you are too busy. You have to stop being busy and start being a priority.

98. Understanding your decision isn't complex at all. You show up for yourself because you are worth it or you don't because you aren't. It is as simple as that.

99. Look yourself in the mirror and speak these words today: Today I am not going to stress and feel like a mess. I am going to dress up and show up. I am about to tie my loose ends for good.

100. Today, go on a journey that brings your heart joy. Do it, not just because you can, but also because you deserve to have what's best for you for a change.

101. For me, it is not enough to settle for less than I am worth. The heart that keeps me alive, desires more for me.

102. When you make yourself an essential part of your life, every stage of your life becomes a happy place to be.

103.   Look yourself in the mirror and speak these words today: I am not going to make any excuses and let this year escape me. I am going to take it by the horn.

104.   The higher they see you fly, the harder they wish you to fall. I will never be perfect, but I promise I won't ever be less than I can be. So no matter how many times you flag my flaws, your words will never drag me down or keep me down. I simply won't stay fall.

105.   If life gets too tough, slow down, but never stop. Keep going. Keep hoping. Keep improving. Life never stops coming at you.

106.   If you wish for a great life for yourself but don't know where to start in life or what to do in life, start with who you are. Make you a why, and get up because of you.

107.   No matter how tired, fed up, or messed up I feel, there is no quitting in me, just the fire to keep moving forward. My feelings aren't keeping me down today.

108.   It is okay to fail. It is okay to be delayed. It is okay to be demotivated. It is okay to be discouraged. These are all part of the process. But giving up on my progress. Now that is never going to be an option. I deserve more. I expect more. I am worth more. And I am getting it. Period.

109. I don't believe quitting is an option. No matter how tough things get, I trust the process because it is not designed to fail me. It is only designed to teach me which ways will or won't get me through my goals.

110. When you start working on yourself, pretty soon, the where and the what will reveal themselves.

111. You might not fit the category of those who have achieved a great feat in life, you might not look like them, walk like them, smile like them, think like them, or talk like them. But who says you have to look a certain way to be called upon to be one of the greatest? Appearance doesn't make a damn difference to greatness. It is the courage not to fit in but to stand out in the full display of your greatness that makes the unquestionable difference among the greatest of time.

112. Look yourself in the mirror and speak these words today: I am responsible for my health. I am responsible for my mind. I am responsible for my body. I am responsible for my worth and belief. I am responsible for my future. I am responsible for advancement in life. I am responsible to show up for every part of my life making me unhappy right now because I am responsible for the conclusion of the success story I deserve. And I am capable

of changing this version of myself into a better version of myself.

113. Sometimes life will bring you down, just to wake you up. Then it is up to you to get back up.

114. Don't just let the thought of happiness live in your head. Let it show on your body. In your soul. In your mind. Get up and strive for a life to be proud of.

115. Today, get up, get on your knees, pray for what you want, and pursue it. Not many people do this. Be different about what you do and do it without leaving any room for doubt.

116. Don't forget to put your faith in your fight. Say this right now: Lord, I thank you for this graceful day. I thank you for this great health. I thank you for the support in each step I take and for the guidance in each fight, I face. I thank you for your strength in my life. I put my intentions today in your hands. Please give me directions. Please give me more than the sight to see what's in front of me. Please give me the wisdom to help me make better choices today.

117. I bring my A-game every day because I want to B the very best I can be. I must do this for myself. I won't rest my best. I am proud of who I am. I am proud to know that I am not who I use to be. And I am proud of what next I can become. I

am proud to keep this up for as long as I can get up. I always get up.

118. Recognise when to call it a day if it drains the life out of you. If you can't fix what's broken, build something much better than what was. Don't waste another breath or energy on a hopeless outcome.

119. Today you have two choices both of which you are capable of making. Either you work hard and end your hardship or you don't and accept your hardship.

120. Once you wake up, what you do or don't do next is a decision.

121. To change what isn't working in your life, you must change what you have been doing so far about it. Habit is the master key to change.

122. If no one has told you this today, it is my pleasure to tell you this: you are an amazing person. You are a box full of remedies and discoveries. Don't settle for fear, don't settle for being average. Have the courage to believe in yourself and have the urge to break the cage of fear and uncertainty.

123. The moment I stopped feeling like a victim in my life and started taking responsibility for what is happening, I also stopped feeling paralysed to create results within it. And through

that, I started believing in my ability to make anything happen.

124. You are too tired today to get up and get on with your goal? Suck it up, get up, and show up. If you don't stick to showing up, you will never change your life for the better.

125. Today is the first stone to the build-up of your best life. Don't leave it out.

126. I am not a morning person but if showing up early than the rest is what it takes. I will be that person. I must pull myself up. I must push myself forward. I will persevere at any cost.

127. Every struggle is an opportunity for you to grow stronger, to become powerful. To become healthier. To reach a new financial high. You just have to accept the challenge, not run from it.

128. If you are struggling with doing enough today, do a little. Everyone can do a little bit. It is better to take one step a day than to stay stuck in a place that you've outgrown for a year. A step each day is better than no steps all year.

129. No one is born negative or positive, but we are born with the capacity to be. We are all born with the capacity to adjust to the world as we are sold it. And we do so through the aid of external opinions, ideas, beliefs, and experiences which all affect our thoughts. Everything around us shapes

everything within our mind and as we grow older, we learn to adapt, reject or accept them as our own. What we experience, we simply turn into expectations and emotions. This is to say, our mind is a mimic machine. It mirrors what it has been conditioned to. Our mind is the only part of our body that can change (subconsciously or consciously) completely. This is good news as a negative mind is not a permanent state of being. But for us to instigate such a positive change, we can only do so through conscious reprogramming. Through repetition, our mind takes the shape of what it's exposed to.

130. To evolve in life, you must have an expectation of who you want to be and where you want to be and let it create a new excitement to wake up to. Then show up daily and see to it that it becomes your new reality.

131. Showing up each day is like taking steps. And steps make the insurmountable become reachable. So stop looking at how far you must go, and focus on getting further ahead each day. That is the only way to get ahead: one step at a time. One step ahead of another step.

132. No one knows you better than you. No one can help you without knowledge of yourself. So you have to extract information to be able to help yourself. And you do so by simply sitting in a quiet space and self-reflecting peacefully.

133. First, work out what you want in life. Then, work out why you want it. Next, work out what you need to achieve it. Then work on it to make it happen. That is how success will show up for you.

134. Staying ahead in life is not about speed but consistency. It is not about anyone, it is about no one but you. You see, somebody will always be ahead of you, and someone will always be behind you. However, if you are careless in your consistency with moving forward, the one behind you will become ahead of you.

135. No matter how much darkness turns up in your life, remember this: Stopped stressing over what's not working in your life. Stop worrying about how strong the darkness is becoming. You can handle anything that life throws at you. You are an excessive force of light. Nothing can oppress the mighty light within you. You are blessed with greatness.

136. To manifest anything, we must first visualise it. Secondly, we must feel deserving of it. And thirdly, we must acknowledge the value it will bring to our life if it were to happen. Then lastly, we must put our perseverance into play in an unmatchable state of consistency to make it happen.

137. What is the worst that can happen if you choose yourself? Your job might fire you. Your friends might leave you. Your lover might leave you. What is the worst that can happen if you don't put yourself first? You are guaranteed to lose losing yourself alongside everything else eventually.

138. Don't be scared of failure. Don't be scared of defeat. Defeat is designed to text you, and to transform you into the powerful version you can be. Defeat will teach you about the strength of your opponent, whatever or whoever it might be, and also help you recognise how to be better prepared next time you face that same battle that you've lost.

139. Don't try to be like everyone else. Be yourself. And be the very best at it.

140. You can either accept life as it comes or make life what you want it to become. The choice is yours to make.

141. While you are working hard to be the best version of yourself. Learn to appreciate everything you are. The good and the bad. Be proud that you are strong enough to accept both of them as your own. And be proud that you are working on being the best good you can be.

142. Sometimes you just have to keep on going even when you think you aren't winning.

Sometimes you just have to keep on going even when you think nothing is showing. Your job is to keep showing up. Seeds show up after a while. Fruits ripen when the timing is right. Trust the process and wait your turn to rise. Just like everything that rises does when the time is right.

143. Stop spending all your day scrolling and liking people's lives. Instead, start sowing into yours so you can live as you desire.

144. I know that is hard to wait any longer when what you deserve is long overdue to you. But what is due won't keep you long waiting in the queue of receiving. Just keep showing up and keep doing what you do. The process of planting and harvesting never fails.

145. As you work on your goal today, don't be discouraged that it hasn't happened yet. Keep going. Be patient with your progress, proceed, and believe in the process. It might not happen overnight or in an instant, but I assure you, it will happen for you soon enough. Your time will come.

146. It gets difficult when you get closer to your goal. So, just when you feel like giving up, that's when you must go on. That's when you must level up. That is when you must turn up the heat.

147. Yes, some people are capable of enhancing your experience of happiness. But no one is or

can become the true source of your happiness. That is all you. So stop looking for what you have the power to give to yourself freely.

148. No excuses can make an exception to quit to those who want an excellent and exciting life.

149. You will never need validation, from anyone if every day you make it a habit to be the first person to recognise your existence and appreciate who you are becoming.

150. When you feel lost, know that you are not lost. On the contrary, you are just on a path unknown that leads to a path to your own glow.

151. No time is convenient to start working on your goals but we must make an exception for what is important to us if it will benefit our life. And right now is an opportune time to start.

152. Hesitation is one way to tolerate what you don't deserve.

153. Not every day is going to be a good day. But you can be good on any day if you keep a positive heart.

154. To appreciate happiness, you have to understand the hurt. This is why you are going through what you are going through while wanting to be happy.

155. Do what you need to do now with ease so you must not have to do it under pressure.

156. You can only improve yourself by providing yourself with why you haven't so far. And then adjusting those habits.

157. When life interrupts, we must do well to intervene.

158. I have come to a point in my life where after looking for someone to blame for where I am today that I don't want to blame. The only one present and responsible is me.

159. I learned a beautiful thing about reward, it comes from the ugly work many are refusing to put in.

160. Today, don't put me in your plan. I am busy. Fully booked directing a story. My success story.

161. I will never see myself give up. Tired or fired up, either way, I will get up. No matter what, I will turn up, for what I want to show up. I mean it this time around.

162. No matter how busy your day is, don't let your lights out too easily. Don't let your day's candle burn down without discovering a new strength, a new perspective, or a new surge of energy. If you search within yourself you will find out something that wasn't there the day before.

163. To get there you have to leave here. Here as in that fear in your mind. Here as in that doubt in your heart, the discouragement, the denial, and the comfort zone.

164. I have no time for distractions or procrastination. This year is for transformation and manifestation. For creation and elevation. Nothing less. Watch out for proof.

165. Don't be a victim of a bad day. Doing so puts the fate of your whole life on the outcome of one bad day. Stay wise.

166. Do what makes you feel alive, not what keeps others in your life.

167. Talk less, do more. Don't say much. Prove it. Let the outcome of your effort explain your attitude.

168. No effort put into you is small. Every building is a collection of little bricks put together over time, not overnight. But no effort is invested in you, that is how you stay exposed and vulnerable.

169. Today be the first good energy you surround yourself with by finding the courage to say no to negativity. You do have the power to empower yourself. You just have to stop focusing on the negative in your life for a change.

170. Prepare daily for what you want to appear in your life one day. You see, where there is a purpose, there must be preparation. Where there is preparation, there is a plan, where there is a plan, there is a pattern, where there is a pattern there is organisation, where there is organisation there is clarity, where there is clarity there is control. In other words, to have control we must be sufficiently prepared.

171. We get up for what we want and we stay in bed for what we still want. Getting up on any day and working on what we want is not a thing of feeling, nor is it of talent, it is a thing of mindset.

172. Often all we see is a success. We don't see the storm. We don't see the sweat. We don't see the struggle. We don't see the moments before the breakthrough. But success is a private process. Success is not an overnight process, same as every seed has to disappear for a while before it appears. So must those also with goals in life. So, are you ready to do the work during your dark times to bloom as if you never went through a dark time?

173. Never let what you've lost cloud your sense of gratitude. Things come and go. But more comes only through the constant appreciation of what you've still got left and not the constant expectation of what you want next.

174. When you have a purpose in life, you wake up differently than everyone else. You wake up ready to rise. You wake up determined. You don't wake up tired of your life; you wake up fired up to transfer it.

175. Many of us are due for a blessing but delayed by the fear of what if it won't work, they are right, it is not the right time, but maybe when I have more. But, As soon as we push forward nevertheless, we are bound to be blessed.

176. Growth does not start because you wish for it or because you ask for it or because you deserve it. Growth starts when you start. It starts when you challenge yourself by taking that first step out of your comfort zone.

177. This mess you are in right now is the right path to your wellness. Don't try to divert yourself from it. Don't try to escape it. Don't try to hide away from it. Embrace it. Take your time if you must, but Face it, Walk through it. And watch yourself glow when you get to the other side of it.

178. It is not really about how you feel right now that wins the day for you. It is about how what you want will make you feel if you go on and make it happen. What's it going to be now? Do something impactful or waste this day?

179. Don't let your emotion get in the way of your progression. Don't let it get in the way of

what will make you proud. Do it because you need to do it. Do it because you believe you deserve more in life. Happiness often comes from doing the things you never did before because you hated doing it.

180. When you show up and put effort into yourself every day, you begin to eliminate a temporal problem that would have evolved and existed permanently in your life.

181. In practice, there are no excuses, just choices. We will always find a way if it matters. Does it matter? Do you matter? It is always on you to make the right choices for you.

182. To be rewarded with what you want you must be willing to sacrifice what you enjoy to do but can survive without doing it.

183. Go harder or stay helpless? I choose to go harder. No room for weakness today.

184. Today is your possession. You can do whatever with it. Make it matter for you.

185. Plan plus performance plus consistency equals progress

186. Today, pay more attention to your output than the outcome you desire, for your desired outcome depends on your delivery.

187. One thing the average person hates the most is staying disciplined. But it is the one thing

that brings successful people to what they want and love.

188. When it comes to achieving your goals, there is nothing more reassuring than putting in the hard work. There is no growth in comfort, just excuses, and excuses will only deny you growth.

189. I can't wait to get up and work on my goal is a strong indicator that your greatness is loading. And faster by each minute of every day!

190. The only miracle you need today is acknowledging that you can make anything you want to happen if you work daily on it. That is the only way to pull it out of the hat. But first, you have to believe in the magic of your own mind.

191. I hope you understand that giving up won't help you glow up. You are built to withstand, the toughest test in your life.

192. Sometimes to change the sad story of your life you have to be the new chapter in it and then, become the best story in it.

193. You are the only person standing in between what you wish for and what you get. Either you show up for your goals in life or you shut up about your life failing you. You don't get to be in your way and have your way.

194. It is just you and the obstacle in your way today. Only one of you can win. But it is up to you if it will be you or not.

195. It doesn't matter what other people think, they can call you selfish or heartless but, Sometimes, other people have to be put on hold and you have to be selfless with yourself to get out of the mess in your life.

196. Be a wise woman before you seek to be a free woman. Be a better man before you seek to be a wealthy man. It is the formal that provides the latter. It is the formal that sustains the latter.

197. Each day you take a step forward you become a better version of yourself. So, No matter what keep going, so you can keep growing. Even if slow is all you can do, go slow, and don't stop. When you quit you become the person you no longer are. Or worse.

198. You can't be lazy and be ahead in life. Life happens so fast, and the lazy always fall behind in life. The only way to keep up is to keep showing up.

199. No matter how long it is taking, don't be discouraged. Keep at it. It will soon show up for you like you have been showing up for it.

200. It is dangerous to keep putting off what you must work on, for your happiness usually depends

on your resolve. So today, work on what you don't want to see anymore tomorrow.

201. To persevere one day, you must wake up with a consistent, persistent, and resistant mindset every day! You have to embrace the journey, whatever it brings. When you meet fear and doubt, which is inevitable, you have to stand tall and say; I defeated you yesterday. And today, don't think I won't do it again.

202. Not everyone is going to understand why you are doing what you are doing. It is for you, not for them. So don't be upset if they think you are crazy. Let your result do the explanation.

203. Learn to embrace your life experiences, good or bad. Everything you go through has a purpose in your life. Yes, in life, the same thing happens to everyone, but some things happen, just for you. And when it does, it can be for one of these reasons: to make you stronger, to make you wiser, to make you cautious, or to make you proud.

204. Some days we are going to get it right. Some days we are going to get it wrong. The most important thing is to show up in a learner's mindset. That way, every step, good or bad, becomes a tool that takes you further into your desired growth.

205. Do not let anyone push you away with their unbelief about your ability to achieve your dream. Their opinion is irrelevant, and your dream is valid.

206. Don't wake up late and rush into a life that crushes you, day in and day out. Give yourself a time-out from burins out. Give yourself the pace and space to wake up early to rest, to reset and to heal.

207. Find what lights you up and let it guide your heart through the dark fortress of life.

208. There is no magic more powerful than hard work. If you want to win anything in life, you have to show up for it and work hard for it.

209. If you are willing to get up early before everyone else and willing to show up despite everything else. Then you are on the right part to living your best life. There is no limit on how far you can reach.

210. Show up and pick up where you left off so you can get to where you failed to get to before.

211. I learned that we won't grow until we want it bad enough. We won't grow until we make it matter. We won't grow until our discomfort outweighs our comfort. We won't grow until we are desperate to depart from our dreadful life. Are you there yet?

212. Explore and discover your purpose in life. Don't stay in a corner in life when you can go further in life. Otherwise. Life will leave you where death will find you.

213. Some days your light will flicker when the storm gets thicker. When those days come, take shelter in your courage, that's your natural shield against any storm.

214. Wise men and women don't live a life that allows them no joy. Be wise. Always go for joy.

215. Don't wait for the light before you start growing. The light will find you on your way to the top, said the soil to the seed.

216. You don't win and shine by whining, wishing, waiting, wobbling and wondering through life. You do so through working hard.

217. Don't stop chasing a better life because everything is going well for you right now. All good things always come to an end. Take more chances in life. Sometimes the good is not always the best you can get.

218. Don't worry about how long it will take. Don't worry about why it hasn't happened yet for you. Your time will come. Just keep turning up. Keep working hard. Give it your all.

219. You can't be chilling and be winning. You can't be sluggish and be ahead in life. If you want

something bad enough, you make it matter. You make time for it. you show up for it. You keep at it and give it your all until it happens.

220. If you are not waking up for yourself, you are not living your life to its full potential. The delay doesn't mean denial. Be on track but don't force your progress. Don't try to do it quicker than you can do it better. The best things in life take time.

221. I know it is not easy to start afresh or to reach the finishing line. But trust in your turn.

222. Some days when nothing shows up, you might feel like the only option left is quitting. But do not buy into it. Keep going. Keep pushing forward. Keep looking forward to a better outcome. Your day of victory will come.

223. This is not the time to doubt yourself. This is not the time to distract yourself. This is not the time to deny yourself. This is not the time to disagree with yourself. This is the time to drive yourself. This is the time to direct yourself. This is the time to deliver yourself to the finish line of your goal. Get up and make it happen.

224. Don't. Panic when life attacks you. Be calm. When you are calm nothing can break down your wall of resistance.

225. If you try to tackle an obstacle with a negative mindset you will never overcome it.

226. Progress starts with the little parts we are willing to play, with the little steps we are willing to take, with the little sacrifices we are willing to make, with the little knowledge we are willing to add on, with the little resistance we are willing to advise ourselves to take, with the little pain we aren't willing to skip, and with the little comfort we are willing to forsake for the greatest pleasures life had to offer.

227. Stop chasing people whose presence makes no substantial positive difference to your mental health. Sometimes it is not the people in your life but the people vacant from your life that restore your peace of mind.

228. The success formula is simple. Intention plus effort equals reward. Expectations plus excuses equal disappointment. You owe no one an explanation or an excuse. Whatever will make you happy, go for it. Do it for yourself. Do it because you can. Do it because you deserve it.

229. Happiness is a decision and it starts with the courage to act according to your heart's demand. Courage is the ability to overrule fear with a decision. To pick what's best for you over what scares you away from doing what's best for you.

230. There is no smile where there were no struggles. It is what we've been through that makes us unbelievably stronger.

231. There is really no perfect way to live life well. To be well, good decisions are necessary but so are mistakes too. But what is better than seeking a perfect existence is experiencing happiness each day that you are alive.

232. This is a year of less compassion and a year of more action. Get up for it and you will get it. Don't and you will regret it. It is as simple as that.

233. It took me some tough years. it took me some painful choices. It took me some challenging sacrifices. But after showing up without fail, those years made me proud of myself.

234. There is nothing impossible about your goal. You have the power to pave your own way. You have the power to call your own shots. You have the power to write your own story. Don't let anyone tell you otherwise not even you.

235. Your goal is as real as your heartbeat. Not everyone will see what your heart and mind can see. So, you are liable to see what's possible where others see failure, impossibility, unlikelihood, limitation, or emptiness.

236. You don't get to the other side, the winning side by building a wall to keep the storm out. You don't get what you want by staying safe and treading water. You don't get to your destination by hesitation. You have to cross the line of doubts, fear, what ifs to get to the finish line, your goal.

237. Count on yourself no matter the odds. Favour favours those who favour themselves as opposed to the opinion of others.

238. Don't lack in the things that will make you look lucky to others. Don't lack in hard work. Don't lack in knowledge. Don't lack in courage. Don't lack in your energy. Don't lack in working out. Don't lack in kindness and generosity. Don't lack in having a good time. Don't lack in wanting better. And don't lack in giving your best.

II

Peace

All the riches in the world are helpless and meaningless on a death bed. But, those who are at peace in live are the healthiest and wealthiest among the rest, even the richest.

PEACE

Not experts, not novices but only steady hands cut straight through the thick log with ease.
To be steady-handed is to be mentally at peace.
To have a steady day is to cut through the thick log of life with ease.
Ease is peace.

So, how at peace are you today? 5am is not merely about productivity. 5am is about having a peaceful daily experience of life.

Truth be told: every day is a mental battle and not just a physical one. And one way to measure if we are winning our mental battle is by how at peace we are. Those who are at their happiest and their best have found ways to be at peace with their mind: a healthy mind produces a healthy life.

What's the state of your peace of mind? Or a better question to yourself is this: How at peace am I?

Dictionary's definition of peace:

Peace: Mental or emotional calm.

Peace: A state or period in which there is no war or a war has ended.

So, I believe in addition to the above definition, to be at peace is to dominate your mind and your life. When we are sad, anxious, depressed, or stressed, it is more often than not an indication that something is happening in our life that we have no control over, and when we have no control, it disrupts our sense of happiness. When we have no peace, we are on the verge of being dethroned from being in control of our life: We are on the losing side of the war in our minds, and daily. To regain/maintain our throne, we must focus on gaining back control. We must simply be at peace.

Productivity Vs Peace

For many of us, getting up at any time even at 5 am is seen as a time for high performance and high productivity. Great stuff! But, is life really all about achievement and possessions, or the memories of experiencing moments of emotional joy and peace in the most exhilarating ways possible to mankind?

A student said to me one day, "But when you get up early to do more, you produce more."

"Yes, that's accurate. But to a degree," I added. "You see, the seduction of fancy possession has taken us away from experiencing the priceless, authentic, admiring, pleasure of life. And, yes, more time leads to more productivity. But, the pleasure of such a way of living has a short shelf life. In the long run, when you get up to produce more, without a positive mindset and peace of mind, it means that you are rushing to get somewhere at the expense of your mental health, and the enjoyment of your physical life. To be at peace is like killing two birds with one stone. Of course, I understand that more performance leads to more productivity. But the rush to produce in quantity is no better than wasting raw materials in the ocean. We perform at our best when we are calm, collected, and at peace. And we can't be at peace and be in a rush at the same time. You can't have both. You can only be one at a time." I concluded.

He nodded and took notes.

For many of us, it seems like the more we have, the sadder we become. The more we do, the gloomier we feel. "What more can I do?" Someone asked me one day.

I looked up and said. "You are asking the wrong question, sir. Your problem is not doing more. Your problem is this: You are not asking yourself the right question."

He waited in anticipation, ready to take note.

The right question is this: Why am I doing more than I am more? Shouldn't achieving more possessions make me happier? More at peace? More stress-free? More excited? More chilled? More healthy?

Some years ago, like many nowadays, I was moving on all cylinders, like an engine: I was doing my master's degree, I was a senior manager, I owned my own business, I was a father, a mentor, a friend, and a partner. But I was not the happy, and at peace self I am today. But why? I mean I was getting up at 5 am. I was way up before anyone I knew. And yes I was getting more done. And yes I was achieving more, and getting to the best places in life I never was able to get to before I started waking up at 5am. But I quickly learned that life isn't all about GETTING to the best places in life physically, but also about BEING in the best place in life emotionally and mentally.

I was a workaholic and a mental mechanic. As a workaholic, I was working more to get more done. As a mental mechanic, I felt like I had to fix everything I failed at when getting things done. In retrospect, it was a vicious circle of madness and a meaningless and tasteless way of living. I simply prioritised my possession over my peace. And I suffered dearly for it.

But After facing an emotional breakdown, and in physical health, I learned that possession is worth nothing if you have neither time nor peace to enjoy it. If you are always looking to get back to work with every single moment to earn more, you are not living your best life. Instead, you are just leaving out the best part of your life just to be a slave to the collection of possessions and by so doing merely rushing towards your doom's day, where every material thing gained becomes nothing but in vain. You lose the best part of your life and suffer for it in health and memorial regret.

Now when teaching about balancing productivity and mental health, I ask people this: What's the point of being mentally unhealthy, suffering from anxiety, stress, and depression but having flashy possessions? Your material possessions are bad therapists. They fade into the background of your fight for your mental health during your period of mental war. Your possessions are powerless when you are in a mess because they can't help you during the dark period of your life. Possessions don't look good in the dark. They don't look like they even exist during your moment of mental war. Your possession simply looks like a valley that holds empty.

I have been dying to ask, but what's the best way to start my day peacefully and of course productivity also? A friend asked me after hearing about my work on the title of the book. I believe there is no one best way to start. But this is how I would start. This is how I start my day peacefully which has proved very productive likewise. And you might want to do the same and then adjust it to your preference later on where necessary.

First thing first, have a designated quiet place in your home you can call your morning place. My quiet place is a place with no distractions, an analog spot: No mobile phones. No TV remote. Just a Table lamp and a cup of something hot.

So, the day before set your alarm earlier than five to give you time to freshen up and be at your spot by 5am. Once I have freshened up, I make myself a hot drink, and then I ensure I am punctual at my spot at 5 am. Then I do nothing but meditate for 10 minutes. I believe if I don't have 10 minutes to give my mind, I can't expect it to give me anything nice for the rest of the day.

Meditation to me is the art of doing nothing but existing in quietness and stillness. Switching off from the dos, and the must-dos of life. Meditation is my way of elevating my peace level so I am in a position to increase my energy and productive level throughout the day. Through engaging in a meditative state before anything else is how I stay in control of my mind: by channeling my inner peace through thinking about nothing, but feeling the purity, quietness, and stillness outside and within me.

Next, I open my notebook and engage in a conscious practice of positive thoughts. I go about it by physically mapping out what I can do, things to avoid doing, and people to connect or not to engage with, to ensure that my day runs as smoothly and stressless as possible in a way that it benefits me emotionally, and not just materially.

Once that is sorted. I engage in a quick workout that mostly involves me stretching my body. A subtle exercise, in particular, one that involves stretching my limbs, has benefited me during my creative moments.

Finally, I open my agenda for the rest of the day. This usually consists of my plan for the day. I always ensure that I have a plan before I wake up. Meaning, I prepare something the day before for the next day. Now, all I have to do is expand on it or make it more vivid and specific. Once those are sorted, I focus on executing my plan with a positive mindset.

I hope that though this last chapter you now understand why your wellness is paramount and why the greatest pleasure in life isn't found in our possession but in moments that bring us peace. So, my final advice before you get on with the rest of your life is this: Wake up for your health before you do for your wealth. Don't be in a rush to have much in life. First, find peace within you before you find things that are outside of you. Learn to find the balance between what you have and how you are. When you get up at 5 am, be that friend that asks you how are you, not one that reminds you of how much more you need to do to have more.

The end of any inspirational story is always the door to a great new beginning. This moment you are in right now is the key to getting through that door.

There are real-life stories we
are destined to write.
This one is mine.

There are real-life stories that our great
destiny needs us to read.
This one is yours.

Ingram Content Group UK Ltd.
Milton Keynes UK
UKHW022229050723
424591UK00014B/502